Union with God:
the teaching of St John of the Cross

By the same author:

Learning about Private Prayer

Union with God:

the teaching of St John of the Cross

by

Desmond B. Tillyer

MOWBRAY
LONDON & OXFORD

Copyright © Desmond B. Tillyer 1984

ISBN 0 264 66934 7

First published 1984
by A.R. Mowbray & Co. Ltd,
Saint Thomas House, Becket Street,
Oxford, OX1 1SJ

Typeset by Midas Publishing Services Ltd, Oxford
Printed in Great Britain by Biddles Ltd, Guildford

British Library Cataloguing in Publication Data

Tillyer, Desmond B.
  Union with God.
  1. John, *of the Cross, Saint*
  I. Title
  248.2'2'0924   BX4700.J7

ISBN 0-264-66934-7

For
A.R.C.

Contents

Foreword by the Bishop of London   ix

Introduction   1

1. Who was St John of the Cross?   4

2. Foundation Principles   15

3. Things Divine   21

4. Things Human   38

5. The Path to Union: First Steps   62

6. The Path to Union: Making Progress   72

7. The Path to Union: Diversions and Distractions   84

8. The Path to Union: Journey's End   104

Bibliography   111

Foreword

by the Rt Revd and Rt Hon. Dr Graham Leonard,
Bishop of London

I am very glad to be given the opportunity of commending this book, for a number of reasons.

In the first place, it is a good book. Fr Tillyer allows St John of the Cross to speak for himself and does so in a way which encourages the reader to turn to the writing of St John himself. Although the teachings of St John are timeless, the terminology which he uses is unfamiliar to most people at the present time. An explanation of it is essential if he is not to be misunderstood and Fr Tillyer provides this admirably.

Secondly, it is a good book about a matter which is central to the Christian life, namely, growing in union with God through prayer. In recent years, there has been a recovery of interest in prayer but all too often the impression has been given that it is a spiritual exercise to satisfy man's desires, which can be pursued simply with a degree of application, rather than the means by which through costly consecration of his whole being to God for God's sake, a person achieves his true destiny. It is for this reason that the teaching of St John is also urgently needed today. At the same time, anyone who expounds it has to contend against the commonly held view that St John is harsh and inhuman and, without minimizing the demands of prayer which he reveals, make it evident that it is precisely because of his love and concern for created humanity that he seeks to guide it to its true end of union with God, which leads to a new and better joy in what is created. Fr Tillyer also does this admirably.

Thirdly, it is a good book about a central matter of the Christian life by a parish priest who I know has a deep love of souls. It springs from loving obedience to the command given at his ordination to do all that lies in him to 'bring' all who are committed to his charge '...to that ripeness and perfectness of age in Christ'. I rejoice that such a book and on such a fundamental matter should have been written by a parish priest of the diocese.

I hope and pray that it will be widely read and used, particularly by those who have the cure of souls and who are asked to give spiritual direction.

17 August 1983   +GRAHAM LONDIN:

In order to arrive at having pleasure in everything,
Desire to have pleasure in nothing.
In order to arrive at possessing everything,
Desire to possess nothing.
In order to arrive at being everything,
Desire to be nothing.
In order to arrive at knowing everything,
Desire to know nothing.
In order to arrive at that wherein thou hast no pleasure,
Thou must go by a way wherein thou hast no pleasure.
In order to arrive at that which thou knowest not,
Thou must go by a way that thou knowest not.
In order to arrive at that which thou possessest not,
Thou must go by a way that thou possessest not.
In order to arrive at that which thou art not,
Thou must go through that which thou art not.

THE WAY NOT TO IMPEDE THE ALL

When thou thinkest upon anything,
Thou ceasest to cast thyself upon the All.
For, in order to pass from the all to the All,
Thou has to deny thyself wholly in all.
And, when thou comest to possess it wholly,
Thou must possess it without desiring anything.
For, if thou wilt have anything at all,
Thou hast not thy treasure purely in God.

(As. I, 14, 11-12)

Introduction

This book is written to provide encouragement to those who seriously desire to pursue their spiritual life within the Christian tradition. Those who read it are assumed to be seeking union with God, and willing to take practical steps towards that goal.

All mystical theologians base their work on the principle that sound spiritual direction depends upon a proper understanding of the stages to union, coupled with a correct assessment of the state of the soul under direction. Failure of directors to grasp this principle leads to serious spiritual damage, possibly even to the point of loss of faith, for those under direction. We need a guide to lead us along the way, pointing out the pitfalls and encouraging us to look ahead to our goal. Among such guides there stands the incomparable figure of St John of the Cross. His writings on the subject have never been surpassed in either accuracy, clarity or comprehensiveness, and it is the purpose of this book to set out his teaching in the form of a primer. It has no greater intention in view than to present his work to the reader in such a form that he or she is able to enter the conceptual world of St John and discover in outline the steps to union with God which the saint presents so richly and so adroitly. This book is not a substitute for St John's writing but a small appetizer to encourage the reader to seek fuller satisfaction from the saint's own works.

The structure of the book reflects this fact. The introductory chapters are very brief. Others have written biographies of the saint and general outlines of the foundation of spirituality. Also, there is no section on the scriptural roots of the spiritual life. Again, others have fulfilled that task admirably. The short bibliography indicates other sources here for the interested reader. Instead, the bulk of the book is an attempt to present in outline the theological and psychological concepts which St John applies to his exposition of the way to union with God, open to all who take the spiritual life seriously. However, it is

1

not to be treated as a detailed guide to the reader's own spiritual state, to be applied without the help of a director well versed in the cure of souls. No book can do that, let alone one which has intentions as limited as this one.

Throughout the exposition, I have taken care to remain within the guidelines set out by St John, wishing to be a follower, not an innovator. To this end, I have quoted extensively from his two principal systematic works, *The Ascent of Mount Carmel* (*As.*) and *The Dark Night of the Soul* (*Dk. Nt.*). Also there are quotations from *The Spiritual Canticle* (*Sp. Cant.*) and *The Living Flame of Love* (*Lvg. Fl.*), but these are fewer than from the first two, because although they conform to them in teaching, these latter books are more lyrical and therefore generally less useful for concise quotation. Because both *The Ascent of Mount Carmel* and *The Dark Night of the Soul* are unfinished, I have been forced to express my own opinions on a couple of issues, but I hope that this is made clear in the text.

Throughout the book, I have used the translation of St John's writings made by E. Allison Peers under the title, *The Complete Works of St John of the Cross*. (*Wks.*) published by Burns Oates & Washbourne, and I would like to thank the publishers for their permission to reproduce the text. All quotations can be identified by the abbreviations set out above beside the titles; Roman numerals refer to book or stanza, Arabic numerals to chapter or verse. Although I have not quoted from the book, I also acknowledge my indebtedness to *The Crucible of Love*, by E.W. Trueman Dicken, one of the most thorough analyses of the Carmelite tradition published in recent times. I am grateful to the staff of St George's House, Windsor, for encouraging me to write the research project on St John of the Cross, initially for the Mid-service Clergy Course of January 1982, which has been the immediate source of this book. In addition, I would like to thank the many people who, in so many different ways, have helped and encouraged me, especially Dr Martin Israel, Ivy Goodley and Joy Thompson. I wish to express my special appreciation to the Bishop of London for agreeing to write the foreword. Also, my thanks are due to Ann Graham for so generously typing out the draft manuscripts and the final copy. Above all, this book is a small personal offering to almighty God in gratitude for his grace and guidance in my life through the writings of St John of the Cross. For nearly twenty years, he has been to me the single most formative influence in my spiritual life and it is as a disciple that I pray that what I have written may promote in a humble way his influence in the lives of those who read this book and wish to put into practice what they learn.

Desmond B. Tillyer
Easter Day 1984

1. Who was St John of the Cross?

On 28 November 1568, in the small town of Duruelo in Castile, three friars of the Carmelite Order took vows as the founding members of the male branch of the Reform movement known as the Order of Discalced Carmelites. This Reform was the inspiration and life's work of St Teresa of Ávila, already beginning to gain ground among the Carmelite nuns, and the introduction of the Reform to the friars marked a significant extension of its influence. St Teresa, always a person of good humour and direct speaking, described these three as two and a half friars, a reference to the fact that one of them was rather short. That short friar took as his new name in religion Juan de la Cruz, John of the Cross. His companions became Antonio de Jesús and José de Christo. Together, they renounced the mitigation of the 'Primitive Rule' of 1209, subsequently relaxed by Pope Eugenio IV, and promised to live in future by the 'Primitive Rule' without mitigation. Their monastery consisted of only a porch, a room with an alcove and a tiny kitchen, set 'in a pigsty' of a small farm.

This decision to join the Reform movement within the Carmelite Order and the vow taken at Duruelo was the major turning point in the life of St John of the Cross. He was born fairly close by in the village of Fontiveros in 1542, and was baptized Juan de Yepes. His parents were of aristocratic stock but impoverished. His father, Gonzalo, was accountant to richer relatives who were silk merchants. His mother, Catalina, was also of good family but her parents were dead and she had been left unprovided for. They married in 1529. On their marriage, Gonzalo's family rejected him and he was forced to work with his wife as a weaver. They had three sons, Francisco, Juan, and Luis. The children were born into poverty and hard work. Seven years after Juan was born, his father died after a painful illness. His widowed mother, after unsuccessfully giving her eldest son into the care of his uncle at Galvez, taught him, on his return to her, to be a weaver, which remained his trade for the rest of his life. Luis died, probably of malnutrition. Catalina left Fontiveros in 1548 for Arevalo to gain more work and remained there for three years. Juan, now nine, was showing signs of intelligence as well as observing the faith of his mother and brother. In 1551, again out of economic necessity, they moved to Medina del Campo and Juan was sent to the catechism school attached to the Convent of the Magdalena, a free school for poor children, usually orphans. It was a hard life at the school, but not one unknown to a child who had already experienced extreme poverty and deprivation. And more important, he was given a basic education, coupled with Christian teaching, and entered into the beginnings of Christian practice and devotion, building on his experience at home. In addition, he studied at the Jesuit College from 1559 onwards. This college was a centre of Christian humanism and here Juan, already devoted to books, developed a knowledge of philosophy, rhetoric and Latin. After four years, in 1563, at the age of twenty-one, he left the Jesuit College and took the Carmelite habit in the Monastery of Santa Ana in Medina, assuming the name of Juan de San Matiás, to be professed a year later.

The precise origins of the Carmelite Order which Juan joined are shrouded in obscurity. It does not have a great founding father such as St Benedict is for the Benedictines and St Francis for the Franciscans, but instead emerges in the twelfth century as a loosely organized group of hermits living on Mount Carmel in the Holy Land. In c.1154 St Berthold is credited with organizing them into the 'Hermits (or Brothers) of St Mary of Mount Carmel', the first step in the eventual founding of the 'Order of Our Lady of Mount Carmel'. However, it is certainly true that, prior to St Berthold, Byzantine monks had settled on the promontory of Carmel immediately overlooking the sea near Haifa; and continuity has been claimed with Elijah and the sons of the prophets who settled on the mountain. There is a large cave known from ancient times as the cave of Elijah.

The connection with Our Lady is both geographical and

theological. The ridge of Mount Carmel can be plainly seen from Nazareth, a daily reminder to the Holy Family of Elijah and his zeal for the Lord God of hosts. Traditions linking Our Lady and Mount Carmel include one that her birthplace was nearby and another that the Holy Family stopped at Carmel on the way back from Egypt. The themes of Nazareth and the Holy Family have always been a strong source of inspiration to the Order in its devotion to the Incarnation. One of the earliest pieces of written evidence of the connection is in a description by a French pilgrim c.1225 of the hermits' oratory dedicated to Mary at the Spring of Elijah (Wadi-es-Siah) on the seaward slope of Carmel. The writer describes it as a 'very beautiful little church of Our Lady'. The title given to the hermits by St Berthold reinforces the point.

In 1209, these hermits at the Spring of Elijah asked the Latin Patriarch of Jerusalem, Albert of Vercelli, for a rule, and he laid down a discipline of well-tempered asceticism. The rule prescribed absolute poverty, total abstinence from flesh, and solitude. It is this rule which remains the basis of the Carmelite life.

As the thirteenth century advanced, so too did the cause of the Saracens against the Latin Kingdom of Jerusalem. Various crusades from western Europe were unable to stem the tide. In 1244, Jerusalem was finally and irretrievably lost to Islam. The effect of this pressure was to drive hermits from other parts of the Holy Land to the refuge of Mount Carmel. From 1238 onwards, increasing harassment by the Saracens led to the hermits migrating westwards and by the time that the monastery on Mount Carmel was lost with the fall of Acre in 1291, the fledgling order had settled in various countries of western Europe, including Cyprus, Sicily and England.

But the new society which the hermits entered was very different from the one they had left behind on Mount Carmel. Europe was under the influence of the new learning which we call the twelfth century renaissance. There had been a decisive shift away from the old centres of learning in the houses of the Benedictine Order and its reformed offshoots into the new universities. The men of the hour were not from the old monastic tradition but from the new orders of mendicant friars. St Francis and St Dominic had seized the initiative, and the age had moved away from stability and solitude into movement and engagement. The scattered hermits encountered hostility as well as hospitality, and their future was in the balance. Fortunately, one of the first Englishmen to join the Carmelites when they settled in England was St Simon Stock (c.1165-1265), who had probably lived as a hermit as a young man, before the Order arrived. In 1247, he became Prior General of the Order and vigorously pursued a policy of consolidation, obtaining papal approval for changes in the life of the Order necessary to meet the new circumstances in which it found itself. He reorganized the hermits on the lines of the mendicant friars, in order to establish the Order as a viable movement within the life of the thirteenth century Church, and yet at the same time retained the emphasis on solitude and contemplation. St John of the Cross was later to describe this combination of evangelistic effort and withdrawal into solitude as the ideal for the religious life, reflecting as it does the pattern of the life of Christ. Thus the main object of the Order became contemplation, missionary work and theology.

In 1452 an Order of Carmelite Sisters was founded in the Low Countries and spread rapidly through France, Italy and Spain. The nuns followed the same rule as the friars, but were enclosed and devoted themselves more particularly to intercession, especially for priests, by prayer and penance. It was into one of these communities of nuns that St Teresa entered in 1533.

However, Pope Eugenio IV (1431-47) relaxed some of the severities of the 'Primitive Rule' of 1209, permitting the existence of a mitigated observance, and it was the consequences of this decision in the life of the Carmelite houses which led St Teresa to found the Reform movement back to the observance of the 'Primitive Rule', which became known as the Discalced Carmelites.

It was into this tradition and heritage that Juan de Yepes entered in 1563, and which was to be the context of his growth to spiritual maturity for the remaining twenty-eight years of his life. The monastery lived in accordance with the mitigated rule, but we have no details as to how the daily life of this particular community was ordered, beyond the general practice of Carmelite houses at that time.

In 1564, Juan entered the university of Salamanca as an arts student, residing in the Carmelite college attached. He was already dissatisfied with his life as a religious and thinking of a stricter observance. The Carthusian Order was in his mind. In 1567, he was ordained priest and in the same year he met St Teresa in Medina where she was founding a second house of the Discalced Reform. She persuaded him to join the Reform and to give up the idea of becoming a Carthusian. He agreed provided she could set up a house for friars quickly. Returning to Salamanca for a further year, he took a course in theology. The new foundation followed a year later in Duruelo.

Once the three friars of the Reform had taken their vows, they organized their life on the austere and simple lines laid down by the Rule. It was a mixed life, in which a considerable portion of the day and night was spent in the recitation of the choir offices, study and devotional reading, the celebration of Mass and times of solitude. In addition, they evangelized the surrounding countryside, walking many miles to scattered hamlets to visit, preach, and hear confessions. Often they returned home very late for their evening meal. Later on, the Discalced Carmelites were to wear hemp-soled sandals, but the three friars interpreted their title 'discalced' literally and walked everywhere barefoot, even when it snowed. At first, they had intended to grow their own food, but as their name became known in the district, the local people supplied their needs.

But the cramped and derelict state of the little house was inadequate from the start and although the friars were more than willing to endure its rigours, nevertheless they eventually received the offer of a house which they knew they had to accept. This was in a nearby village called Mancera. This house was opened in June 1570, about eighteen months after the start at Duruelo, with considerable splendour, the profession of two more friars and a throng of interested aspirants.

For the next seven years, John of the Cross lives a quiet and obscure life which in hindsight can be seen as a period of silent preparation and growth in maturity. He is first novice-master at Mancera, and then from October 1570, at Pastrana where Antonio de Jesús had inaugurated a second reformed foundation for men. Then a Discalced College was established at the new university of Alcalá de Henares and in the spring of 1571, St John is sent there to take charge of the new venture, and to act as spiritual director to the Carmelite nuns in the city. In the event he stayed little more than a year and, after some comings and goings early in 1572, he was sent as one of two confessors to St Teresa's original convent of the Incarnation, at Ávila, where he stayed, in peace and tranquillity, for five years. As it happened, St Teresa was ordered to return to the convent of the Incarnation in 1571 as Prioress, with the task of restoring some discipline into its life which had become very lax, and for about half the time of his stay, St John was able to work with her in renewing the life of the convent and to share with her his thoughts and aspirations. It is interesting that up till this time we have no evidence that he had written anything, but very soon after leaving Ávila he is known to have begun to write. Maybe it was the influence of St Teresa which gave him the encouragement to do so. Certainly, the violent manner of his departure from Ávila was not conducive to such a new development in his work, and some other even more powerful influence upon him may be supposed.

In December 1577, St John was seized by friars of the Observance in Ávila, opposed to the Reform, and carried off to their monastery where he was flogged twice, further ill-treated and forced to wear the habit of the Mitigation. Then he was moved to Toledo, blindfolded and taken to the monastery of the Mitigation where he was imprisoned and interrogated, along with others, in an attempt to persuade them to abandon the Reform. He refused, despite promises of high office if he surrendered and threats of severe punishment if he did not. St John had become the victim of the political struggle within the Carmelite Order between the Mitigation and the Reform, which was to end in 1580 with the permanent division of the Order.

Placed in a cell measuring ten feet by six feet, with no outside window, only a hole high in the wall connecting it with the large room next door, St John was to remain there for nearly nine months. Except when rarely permitted an oil lamp, he had to stand on a bench to read his breviary by the light through the hole into the adjoining room. He had no change of clothing, a penitential diet of water, bread and scraps of salt fish, and at first

9

he was forced to eat this meal in the refectory, after which he was required to bare his shoulders for the penance called the 'circular discipline' in which the friars would walk around him in a circle, each striking him with a whip and passing it on to the next in order. But he was immovable and eventually the punishment ceased in May.

Added to his physical pain was the psychological torment of the taunt that the Reform was collapsing and how foolish it was of him to hold out any longer. He had no way of knowing the truth, but could only continue upholding his commitment to the Reform without companionship, sympathy or information from outside. All had been taken away except his relationship with God, and it was upon this that he relied at this time of total deprivation.

But from this point of deepest darkness, there was struck a light of such dazzling brilliance that the Church continues to benefit from its illumination. St John begged from his gaolers pen and ink and a small amount of paper, and when they came he folded the paper a number of times to make it into a little book. In this little book, he began to write, and when he escaped from prison he brought with him three poems. We do not know the order in which he wrote them, but their style suggests that he first tried his hand at poetry with a few straightforward stanzas on the theme *In principio erat Verbum*, followed by a second poem, also simple in form, but of greater authority and surer touch, introducing for the first time the theme of the dark night. Then, probably lastly, he wrote the first thirty stanzas of the longest of his poems, entitled *The Spiritual Canticle* and describing the soul in pursuit of the divine lover. The development of his poetic skill and achievement is extraordinary, rising from the fairly pedestrian use of the traditional Spanish form of assonance, through a marked freeing of his style into something more lyrical and finely balanced in the second, into the mature beauty and grace of *The Spiritual Canticle*. St John's burning love for God has turned from scholastic theology to mystical theology as his vehicle of expression and in so doing found release into a gift which has placed him among the greatest of Spanish poets.

After five months' imprisonment, St John's conditions were

10

made a little less desperate. The floggings became only occasional and he was given a new and more kindly gaoler who allowed him freedom to exercise. Eventually one night — whether through the gaoler's co-operation or not is unclear — St John managed to prevent his cell door being securely bolted, and using his bedclothes to form a rope, he let himself down through the window in the adjoining room into the courtyard below. Under cover of the darkness he sought out the reformed convent of nuns in Toledo where he was given refuge. After food, the nuns took him to their chapel where he read to them his three poems. In the meanwhile a canon of the cathedral was summoned, who smuggled the escaped prisoner through the pickets set up by the friars of the Mitigation, gave him fresh clothes and sent him away to the safety of Almodóvar del Campo, south of Toledo, where an important chapter of the Reform was gathering.

To aid his recovery from the ordeal he had gone through, the chapter appointed St John Vicar of Monte Calvario. Also, it isolated him from the political conflict raging between the Reform and the Mitigation. On his way to his new appointment, his recuperation was helped by a stay with the nuns of Beas de Segura, whose prioress Anne of Jesús was one of St Teresa's most loved spiritual daughters. Having met the nuns and found their convent a place of peace, he stayed on this first occasion a few days but returned regularly to visit them during his time at Monte Calvario.

It is from Beas that we have first signs of him expressing himself in prose. Perhaps the nuns asked for a commentary on the *The Spiritual Canticle*; perhaps he had already planned to do so while in prison. In the event, this was the start of his life's work in prose, the commentaries on his three greatest poems. He begins commentaries called the *The Ascent of Mount Carmel* and the *The Spiritual Canticle*. The former was based on his poem the *The Dark Night*, probably composed at about the same time.

Monte Calvario was to prove a short stay for him — after eight months, in June 1579, he was sent to direct a newly established Carmelite College at Baeza, a cathedral city forty miles south, in Andalusia. For St John, this is his first contact as a Castilian with this province and he found himself isolated and alone. At

Monte Calvario he had been able to enjoy the countryside and had taken the novices out to find solitude amidst the natural beauty of the region, and he himself had spent long periods alone in the mountains. Here in Baeza he was less at home in a busy town of strangers and a considerable distance from the nuns at Beas.

But there were compensations, especially in his return to academic life and contact with students. Here his poetry and prose writing continued apace. In June 1580, a papal Bull established the Reform as a separate province, bringing the internecine strife between the two sides to an end. At their first chapter in 1581, Gracián was elected Provincial, and St John was appointed Prior of the monastery of Los Mártires, even further south, near Granada. This new foundation was impoverished and St John had to go out to beg for food for the community, as well as taking his part in the task of actually completing the buildings. Compensation was found in the companionship of Anne of Jesús who had arrived to found a new convent in Granada. Here he continued the *The Ascent of Mount Carmel*, completed the *The Spiritual Canticle* and began the *The Dark Night of the Soul*. In 1585 he wrote the *The Living Flame of Love* in fifteen days of intense inspiration. Neither *The Ascent* nor *The Dark Night* were ever completed. Also in 1585, he was elected Vicar-Provincial of Andalusia and founded numerous new houses in the region. His ability as an administrator and leader of men was demonstrating itself in the organization of the new province as an additional gift to those of artistic merit and spiritual insight.

But this period of growth and consolidation for the Reform was about to be put at risk by an internal conflict which was even less edifying than the previous one between the Reform and their opponents in the Mitigation. In 1585, Gracián handed over his provincialate to Doria, much to St John's surprise. The two had been rivals for a long time and Doria was not a person to brook opposition. Within three years he had deprived Gracián of all his offices in the Order, and a little later caused him to be expelled.

In 1588, St John attended the first Discalced Chapter-General, held in Madrid. At it, Doria was elected first Vicar-General and instituted, not without opposition, a new tribunal of seven to replace the authority formerly held by the priors in chapter. Although seen by many to be contrary to the spirit of the Primitive Rule, the system came into being, among the first consiliarios being St John and Antonio of Jesús, the former prior of Duruelo. By his appointment, in addition, as Prior of Segovia and head of the Congregation in the absence of the Vicar-General, St John became the first of the consiliarios and Doria's second-in-command.

This development made further demands on his administrative talents and his esteem within the Order augured well for the future. However, this was not how matters turned out. As he was leaving for the General Chapter in Madrid, to be held in June 1591, one of the Segovia nuns commented to him that perhaps he would return as Provincial. His reply was, 'I shall be thrown into a corner like an old rag.' At the General Chapter, Doria set out to complete his remodelling of the Reform along his own lines by proposing the revocation of the Teresan Constitution of 1581. Only St John spoke against and his objections were received in silence. Doria triumphed, St John was relieved of all his offices and he left the meeting once more a simple friar. There was a half-hearted suggestion that he might become Provincial of Mexico but that plan was dropped.

He accepted the new state of affairs with resignation and wrote on the same day as his deposition a letter in which he expressed his acceptance of what had taken place, together with a renewed commitment to the will of God. In that letter, he wrote one of his most famous dicta: 'Where there is no love, put love and you will find love.' Not the words of an embittered man, but rather the generosity of one who lives in union with God.

St John was sent into virtual exile, to the lonely friary of la Peñuela, where he was well received and became spiritual director of the community. Freed from his administrative and organizational responsibilities, he was able to seek solitude with nature and with God. He was up before dawn in the countryside; sometimes he spent all night at prayer in the garden. But he was not left entirely alone to find peace. Letters from anxious nuns needed wise replies; news of the way the new constitution was being implemented must have pressed hard on him; the hint of scandal was being stirred up about his dealings with some of the nuns and depositions were being collected in an unjustified attempt to ruin his good name. In all this he remained calm and unmoved, at peace with God and himself.

In mid-September 1591 he became ill, with a fever. Medical treatment was imperative. The choice was either Baeza where he was well-known or Úbeda where he was unknown. He chose Úbeda. The journey there was so draining that he arrived nearly dead, in great pain and exhaustion. The physician diagnosed erysipelas in the foot. There were no comforts to hand and the prior of Úbeda was hostile, even to the point of complaining about his need for food. When the prior at la Peñuela heard he retaliated by sending vast quantities. Also he wrote to the new Provincial, Antonio de Jesús, who came to see his old friend and rebuked the prior for his attitude to the sick man.

The fever grew worse; an operation was performed but without success; the disease spread throughout the body; St John was told that he was dying. He accepted the news, knowing the truth already, and in full consciousness received the Viaticum and prepared for death. By 14 December it was clear to him that death was very near. His last request was for the assembled friars to read to him from the Song of Songs. As the end approached, he lay back with a crucifix in his hands, and waited for the stroke of midnight. As the hour began to strike, he said clearly and simply, 'It is time for Matins,' and died. He was not far short of fifty.

He was beatified by Pope Clement X in 1675 and canonized by Pope Benedict XIII in 1726. In 1926, Pope Pius XI declared him to be a Doctor of the Church Universal.

It is the exposition of the teaching of this great mystic and saint which is the aim and purpose of this book. As such, it cannot do more than convey in barest outline the riches of his teaching and of his powerful personality which animates every page of his writing. To savour the fullness of St John's contribution to the life of the Church, the reader must go to the works themselves. But it is hoped that this book will be of some assistance to those who do so.

2. Foundation Principles

The development of a Christian spirituality emerges out of a commitment to seek after God and a hope of finding him. As such, it requires that we have faith in God and believe that he wants us for himself. Because of our understanding of the nature of God, rooted in God's own revelation of himself as personal, and our awareness of ourselves as personal also, made in the image of God, this quest for God means the bringing together of things human with things divine in a union which is communion and communication, not absorption and extinction. Theology and psychology come together as handmaids of those who set out to seek God, to help them to travel hopefully in the right direction, towards that 'union and transformation of love (in which) the one gives possession of itself to the other, and each one gives and abandons itself to the other and exchanges itself for the other' (*Sp.Cant.* XI, 6). This is our goal, the purpose of our journey, and we shall see how the theology and psychology of St John are combined by him to map out the route we are undertaking. But before we can begin the journey, we need to be aware of the point from which we begin as well as the place we wish to reach. Therefore, this chapter is devoted to considering briefly the relationship between God and ourselves from which we start and which underpins all progress towards union with him.

First, any presentation of spirituality worthy of the name must concern itself with the priority of prayer. God's call to each one of us to pray is fundamental, and we cannot even begin to set out on the road to union unless we accept that every step on the way is a step made in prayer. 'Both the great Carmelite reformers pay close attention to the early stages of the mystical life, beyond which many never pass, and both give the primacy to prayer as a means of attaining perfection. To St Teresa prayer is the greatest of all blessings in this life, the channel through

15

which all the favours of God pass to the soul, the beginning of every virtue and the plainly marked high road which leads to the summit of Mount Carmel. She can hardly conceive of a person in full spiritual health whose life is not one of prayer. Her coadjutor in the Carmelite Reform writes in the same spirit. Prayer, for St John of the Cross as for St Teresa, is no mere exercise made up of petition and meditation, but a complete spiritual life which brings in its train all the virtues, increases all the soul's potentialities and may ultimately lead to "deification" or transformation in God through love' (*Wks.* Vol.I, p.1-2). We are presented here with a far deeper grasp of the meaning of prayer than that usually accepted by beginners. Prayer, for St John, is a source of grace from which flows the means to attempt a complete transformation of life, starting at the bottom and working systematically to the summit of perfection. It follows, therefore, that prayer is the vocation given to us all, from which flow all other vocations, actions and attitudes. To define being a Christian in terms of an approach to life requires of necessity reference to the central place of prayer in our relationship with God, and from that central place a vision of the world seen through the eye of prayer. However, to deduce that spirituality is synonymous with prayer is to produce a simplification which distorts the truth — and which pitches us back into a beginner's understanding of the meaning of prayer.

Spirituality has prayer as its heart, and from that heart there flows a concern for every aspect of life. Nothing human, or indeed creaturely, is outside the consideration of the person who takes spirituality seriously. God's grace upholds creation and transforms it through redemption, and our response to his grace is to be as comprehensive and all-embracing as his graciousness towards us in the first place. Prayer is tested in our practical response to God's all pervasive and transfiguring grace. In short, spirituality is to do with 'life-style', centred on prayer, and working itself out in every facet of existence. Therefore, any exponent of the spiritual life worthy of the name will bring all human activity under the scrutiny of his gaze. All things human are to be brought into a grace-bearing fruitful relationship with things divine.

Secondly, Christian spirituality is concerned with the human race as redeemed. The witness of the scriptures is that we are a new creation in Christ, and it is our status in the presence of God as renewed men and women, adopted children of God, fellow-heirs with Christ, which gives us our starting point for progress to union with him. The redeeming work of Christ gives us the very basis we need for confidence to set out. We begin our quest for union with God, assured that the new relationship secured for us by Christ is unshakable, that 'neither death, nor life, nor angels, nor principalities, nor things present, nor things to come, nor powers, nor height, nor depth, nor anything else in all creation, will be able to separate us from the love of God in Christ Jesus.' Thus, spirituality is not interested in questions of Christian apologetics or Christian dogmatics for their own sakes, but assumes that the person who is seeking God will be conversant with them already, and is prepared to use the truths which they enshrine as the foundation upon which to build a securely founded spiritual life, which expresses and develops that new relationship with God laid down by Christ, our sure corner stone.

And this element of building brings us to the third point to be stressed in this interaction between things human and things divine. The foundation laid is not the completed building. The new relationship between God and us, secured by Our Lord Jesus Christ, does not produce automatic holiness in the individual or immediate union with God. Rather, we experience a progressive relationship with God in which his grace leads us to develop in the direction of holiness and to hope for union. This is simply another way of reminding ourselves of the truth that the grace of God does not distort, override or destroy our human nature, but renews and reforms it gently to bring us into the condition where we are prepared for the vision of God. The transformation of each person into a saint is a task which must be undertaken by the individual, grounded in the secure relationship we have in Christ, and tackled systematically as a co-operative response to the grace of God. There are no short cuts, no instant achievements, no ready made quick results to produce sanctity, only the daily commitment to Christ which gives our life direction and meaning and the daily dedication to working with God's grace which moves us closer to him.

The fourth assumption of Christian spirituality is that the secure foundation laid for us by Christ is received by us sacramentally. St John wrote for those who had been born again in Christ through baptism, and united with him in his death and resurrection. Baptismal regeneration initiates us into his saving acts and brings us their benefits. Here is the means whereby we are given by God the status of redeemed through the new relationship won for us by Christ. This status is renewed regularly in the Eucharist which continues to sustain and nourish us in the life of Christ and to provide us with grace to grow into Christlikeness. Because this sacramental status provides the foundation upon which is built that Christian life which is intended to be completed in union with God, the task of spirituality is to outline the journey between these two related and necessary aspects of the life of grace — between its beginning in baptism and its end in the vision of God.

Fifthly, St John defines the union with God as 'knowing God'. But because the grace of God leads us to union with God through the transformation of ourselves, the task of spirituality is necessarily to lead us not only in the right direction towards knowing God but also in the right direction towards knowing ourselves. To know God and to know ourselves are aspects of the journey which go hand-in-hand and cannot be separated without loss of benefit to the soul. This knowledge, based on the biblical understanding of knowing God, is not intellectual or scientific knowledge, but knowing in a more direct, immediate manner. It is not 'knowing about' or 'knowing of' someone or something, but having intimate personal knowledge of God and ourselves. The root concern is with insight or personal intuitive awareness, not information. What we are being led to is an intimate knowledge of God which is deeper than thoughts and words, concepts and ideas, and therefore remains inexpressible, beyond comprehension, and yet totally penetrating and transforming the soul. This knowledge St John calls 'dark and confused' because it is supernatural in origin, uncreated knowledge of God himself. 'The obscure and general type of knowledge is of one kind alone, which is contemplation that is given in faith' (*As*. II, 10, 4). 'Contemplation, whereby the understanding has the loftiest knowledge of God, is called mystical theology, which signifies secret wisdom of God, for it is secret to the very understanding that receives it. For this reason St Dionysius calls it a ray of darkness' (*As.* II, 8, 6).

It is worth noting that here in this contemplative knowledge of God is fulfilled also the Stoic maxim, 'Know yourself'. The knowledge of God which comes in union with him brings with it knowledge of our true selves transformed into the likeness of Christ. We discover that what we know about ourselves gives way to a deeper intuitive knowledge of ourselves as we really are in God's sight, and our desire to be united in the will with the will of God brings with it the discovery that we know ourselves as we are known in him already. The way ahead is a path to union in which we find our true selves in the very process of finding ourselves united with the true God.

Therefore, although theology — things divine — is not about this kind of knowing, but is rather knowing about God, and although psychology — things human — is not about this kind of knowing, but is rather knowing about our human nature, nevertheless both theology and psychology are indispensable aids in the initial stages pointing us in the right direction. Working together, they clear away many barriers that hinder the beginner's progress along the road and they bar the way to many inviting but erroneous paths and tempting but unsatisfactory short cuts. Both are necessary to the beginner if solid and well-founded progress is to be made.

This does not of course imply that theology and psychology are detrimental influences upon the soul. Quite the opposite. The Christian faith holds as a central cherished conviction that the whole person is created good. Thus, with this faith, we are not asked to reject 'knowing about' in favour of 'knowing', but to let 'knowing about' carry us as far forward towards union as it can, and then to move into contemplation with its attendant transformation of 'knowing about' into 'knowing'. We do not despise or put to one side intellectual insights, but recognise that they are given to us to be used as stepping stones to what is beyond. We are called to leave them behind not because they are not good, but because they are not good enough to carry us all the way to union with God.

The final point of this chapter is the necessary reminder that the journey from beginning to end is one of sensitivity, delicacy and balance. Human beings are created by God with the capacity to seek after him and find him; they reflect his graciousness by being able to become gracious in turn through him. There is here a mysterious intercourse which cannot be described without some loss of immediacy and some impoverishment of experience, no matter how inspired the exponent, even St John of the Cross. Any description of a relationship, whether it be with the self or with another, is always more complicated and less real than the relationship itself. Inevitably any tabulation of St John's thought is to some extent deceptive of its simplicity, while St John's thought is in turn deceptive to some extent of the simplicity of the relationship itself being described. We are twice removed from the Christian experience under consideration. But, having made the point and emphasized the limitations thus imposed on what follows in the next chapters, the exercise remains worth the undertaking, if only to encourage more people to read St John in the original, and then, even more important, to put into practice what he teaches. All spiritual writers warn their readers of the folly of reading their works without the accompanying intention to apply what they learn to their own lives. This warning is worth repeating at this point lest we fall under the condemnation of God as being counted among those who know what they ought to do but fail to seek the grace of God to do it.

3. Things Divine

St John of the Cross is a man of his age, but he is also a Christian standing firmly within the great tradition of the Church and Christian spirituality. He sets out in a systematic manner the experience of the serious person of faith who seeks to live within that tradition, in such a way that it can be understood and appreciated by his readers, and applied to their particular circumstances. He writes not only as a man of his age but also as an author with a particular readership in mind. Therefore in the Prologue to *The Ascent of Mount Carmel* he makes three important preliminary points.

First, St John declares that his writings depend upon holy scripture, 'because he who speaks therein is the Holy Spirit' (*As.* Pr. 2). It is his clear intention that the reader should recognize that he writes under the authority of the Bible and that he has no wish or intention to deviate from its teaching.

Secondly, St John declares that if it is thought that he has strayed from the teaching of holy scripture, either through his own imperfect understanding of the Bible or of other matters not connected with it, i.e. if he has either misinterpreted holy scripture or misapplied it to other things, then he submits his work to 'the sound sense and doctrine of our Holy Mother the Catholic Church' (*As.* Pr. 2).

Thirdly, St John declares that he is not writing for the general public, but for certain of the friars and nuns of the Order of Mount Carmel of the primitive observance (*As.* Pr. 9) whom God is setting on the road to Mount Carmel. This implies two things, namely, that he is writing for a group of people who are thoroughly grounded in Christian doctrine and therefore are well equipped to read a technical treatise, and are serious about pursuing union with God and therefore will benefit spiritually from what they read.

These three points together govern the approach of St John to his writings, and make it clear that, if we are to understand what he is saying, then we have to take his presuppositions into account.

The first point about holy scripture is one upon which Christians can agree. In modern terms, St John is saying that he depends upon holy scripture as containing all things necessary for salvation. However, while the principle is clear, and no Christian worthy of the name would wish to tamper with holy scripture or deny its centrality in the life of the Church, nevertheless, the impact of biblical studies has made the literalist approach to the Bible untenable to all except fundamentalists. In one sense, this gives the reader of holy scripture more scope for interpretation, and therefore, the reader of St John's work may not be impressed by much of his biblical analysis. However, in another sense, this presents the reader of St John's works with a more difficult problem, namely, recognizing any scriptural authority for his exposition of the spiritual life, because of the malaise in the life of the Church concerning the practical day-to-day authority of holy scripture in the lives of individual Christians. The Bible is much less the plumb-line against which the Christian measures his actions than it used to be, and personal opinion supported only by individual likes and dislikes has often been elevated to replace the authority of holy scripture, with the result that it is tempting to ignore St John's firm intention to anchor his spirituality in scripture and to see it instead as one option among many, each assessed according to taste. This could not be further from the mind of St John, or the intention of this book. The clear intention to found Christian spirituality on holy scripture is designed to ensure that it is the guidance of the Holy Spirit which lies at the heart of the approach to God, not simply the idiosyncracies of individual predeliction. This remains a cardinal point in this book as much as it does with St John, even though it is accepted that biblical studies require a more thoughtful and integrated interpretation of the meaning of holy scripture than the old literalist and allegorical approach current previously in the Church.

The second point about the authority of the Church as the arbiter of truth was as vexed an issue in St John's day, as it is today. Reformation thinkers at the time were particularly concerned throughout most of Europe with precisely this point — the nature of the *magisterium* of the church. In the twentieth century, the Roman Catholic Church has been plunged into turmoil by the second Vatican Council, with its consequences in the popular mind of the conflicting claims of ecclesial teaching and individual conscience. The Church of England has long lived under a system of devolved authority, focused in the *ministry, holy scripture*, the *sacraments* and the *creeds*, and has been agitated by the impact of *synodical government* upon these four points of reference. Protestant churches have nailed their colours to the dual masts of holy scripture and individual conscience, only to find that neither has the resources within itself to resolve conflicts between the two of them. St John certainly saw 'the sound sense and doctrine of our Holy Mother the Catholic Church' as residing in the *magisterium* of the Church exercised by superiors in the Order, the bishops, councils and ultimately the Papacy. There was for him a clear chain of command. But for us, the matter is more complex. As an Anglican, I would wish to submit the teaching of this book to the official teaching of the Church of England as set out by authority, by which is meant canonical authority. However, whether or not the reader is prepared to see what is written in these terms is entirely unpredictable. Unlike St John in sixteenth century Spain, there is real difficulty in making any assumption that the reader is part of or accepts the *concensus fidelium*, which makes the opportunities for misunderstanding great.

The third point flows from this. St John wrote for a clearly defined readership. This book must do likewise. However, easy access to books does mean that sometimes what is written with one readership in mind is widely read by another readership not intended or catered for. Therefore, it is important to stress again, as we did at the beginning, that the intention of this book is that it should be for men and women of Christian faith who are committed to seeking union with God and willing to make such sacrifices as are necessary to reach that union. Only a basic grasp of the fundamental articles of faith is assumed; detailed, technical theological expertise is not required. The intention is to re-express what St John has written in language which can be understood by the priest or lay person in the average parish, who is searching for genuine union with God.

To begin this task, it is important to recognize two further factors in St John's writings.

The first is the central place of Christ in his life. His writings are concerned with expounding the path to union with God, and as such read as theocentric rather than Christocentric, but this impression is misleading. The framework of his faith is an orthodox Christological framework. This means more than an acceptance of the traditional understanding of the incarnation and the person of Christ, more than a traditional acceptance of the central place of faith in the birth, death and resurrection of Christ as the saving acts of God by which man is reconciled to God. Over and above these, it means accepting also the consequences of the incarnation and the saving work of Christ, namely that the Christian life is lived 'in Christ', and that this life in Christ is given to us sacramentally and is a participation in the life of God himself through him.

St John writes for those who have been baptized into the death and resurrection of Jesus Christ, dying to sin, knowing forgiveness and rising again to a new life which is the foretaste of eternal life in union with God; for those who have been confirmed with the gift of the Holy Spirit, in whom we progress to Christian maturity which is the measure of the stature of the fullness of Christ; for those who receive regularly the Sacrament of Christ's Body and Blood as 'the medicine of immortality' and food for our journey as we tread the mystic way to union with God. This deeply spiritual approach presents those seeking union with God through Christ with the first step in their pilgrimage of faith along the mystic way. St John assumes that this step has been taken, but the readers of this book may not have done so. To those who have not, St John still offers a vision to excite their faith, a goal to inspire their hope, and a worthy object for their love, even though the fullness of life in Christ has still to be secured through sacramental initiation into him.

Furthermore, the quality of this present living in Christ is that of his own pattern of dying and rising to new life; he writes for those who are willing and eager to take up their cross daily and follow Christ. The grace of this present living in Christ is the

24

source of our faith in God, our hope for God and our love for God; we depend upon the graciousness of his death and resurrection to give us the means of our approach to God. The knowledge of God which we receive through this living in Christ is revealed knowledge of him as the God and Father of Our Lord Jesus Christ; it is Jesus's own relationship with God which he has by virtue of his sonship which shows us what God is like and secures for us our own relationship as his Father's adopted children by baptism.

This centrality of Christ to St John and the whole Discalced Reform can be seen not only by St John's own love of the holy scriptures, especially the gospels, but also the fact that it was at the Convent of the Incarnation that the Reform was first centred, and that when St John and two other friars took the vows of the Reform at Duruelo they chose as their names John of the Cross, Anthony of Jesus and Joseph of Christ. Hagiographers may sentimentalize their names by saying that they wished to know only 'Jesus Christ and him crucified', but there is here the profound truth that all three centred their new life in the Discalced Reform upon the person and work of Our Lord Jesus Christ.

Also, recognizing the central place of Jesus Christ in St John's theology reminds us of the truth that only a Christological framework does justice to both the nature of God and the nature of man. Any theology which attempts to describe God without Jesus Christ is not Christian theology and its vision of God is inadequate to encompass the riches of the grace of Our Lord Jesus Christ. Any psychology which attempts to describe man without Jesus Christ is not Christian psychology and its vision of man is inadequate to describe the measure of the fullness of the stature of man as seen through God's eyes. What St John is presenting to us in his work is a true Christian humanism. He is seeking to excite his readers into the realization that union with God is the transfiguration of man. He is concerned not to destroy or distort our human nature, but to open it up to the grace of God to be transformed into the likeness of Christ who is perfect man. We shall misunderstand St John if we read him with presuppositions which imply that progress towards union with God requires denial of our human nature. St John is concerned not with denying our human nature, but with denying its imperfections so that we gain the freedom to reorder our human nature and align it to the will of God as found in the life of Christ.

The second factor in St John's writings is his grounding in the theology of St Thomas Aquinas, commonly called Thomism. Standing as he does astride the sixteenth century, and educated in theology at the university of Salamanca, St John's theology is expressed in terms of the well-established Thomist tradition, matured and refined by three hundred years of thought and application by scholars. Although St Thomas's philosophy received its characteristics from the metaphysical writings of Aristotle, at a deeper level he continued to uphold many fundamental Platonic and neo-Platonic doctrines handed down in the tradition of the Church from St Augustine and Dionysius the Aeropagite. Indeed St John also read St Augustine and Dionysius first-hand, as well as St Thomas, and together they enabled him to build a secure theological foundation from which he was able to write with such a sure touch upon the path to union with God.

To grasp the importance of the Thomist tradition in the mystical writings of St John we need to consider three principles which St Thomas sets out as the basis to any understanding of the relationship between God and man.

First, the principle of God as non-contingent being and all else as contingent being. St Thomas bases his whole theology on the simple presupposition that God is and we are. The difference between God and all else is that he is independent of all else, but all else is dependent upon God. To be independent of all else is to be non-contingent; to be dependent upon God for one's being is to be contingent. St Thomas posits the objective independent existence of God as a fact and the objective dependent existence of all else as another fact. God is neither an intellectual concept invented and nourished by the mind nor an emotional reaction born and nurtured of the feelings. He is not the product of our human subjectivity, but is a reality objective to the human person. In addition, although all else besides God is dependent upon him and therefore contingent, nevertheless that all else — which we call creation — exists independently

26

of us and shares in the status of being, even though not in the un-created, independent, non-contingent manner which belongs to God alone. We and the world around us are more than ideas in our minds or the products of our feelings; we and the world are existent beings, called to relate to the being of God. There is here in St Thomas a straightforward, matter-of-fact recognition of the ontological reality of God and his creation.

Secondly, St Thomas teaches that faith is distinct from reason. To believe and trust in God is not the same thing as being able to reason oneself to God. Thought-processes get us so far but then falter in the face of incomprehensible mystery. St Thomas draws a clear limit to the claims of philosophy to be able to lead us to God.

This is not to say that faith is unreasonable, or that reason is totally useless in considering the object of faith. Rather, St Thomas sees the matter as a two-stage process. Reason, considering intellectually, and acting naturally upon, the philosophical evidence for the existence of God, is able to reach certain conclusions, but these conclusions do not present a statement about the divine which reason can identify with the God in whom Christians believe. There has to be an initiative from God himself — what we call divine revelation — to show us what he is like in greater clarity than the powers of reason can produce. This is the second stage in the process and to be able to benefit from this second stage, the person seeking God must respond to God's revelation with faith. He has to believe that what is presented to him through the history of God's self-disclosure in the Old Testament and supremely in Jesus of Nazareth is true, in order to come to a fuller knowledge of God. 'I believe in order that I may understand,' says St Anselm, and this is the stance required at this stage of those seeking God.

The further decision to identify the sketchy outlines of divinity as set out by philosophy with the God of revelation is a leap of faith by the believer based on the assumption that while philosophy may be inadequate it can still be accepted as pointing to the truth about God as far as it goes, and that God has given man intellectual ability precisely in order to help him to 'feel after him and find him' so that any search for truth is in essence a search for God who builds upon our natural powers of discernment by revealing himself as consistent with them.

So it is that St Thomas, using the philosophical resources of his time, was able to argue that reason, unaided by revelation, does lead us to an understanding of the divine as one, simple, eternal, good, non-contingent being. But it cannot bring us to the fundamental Christian truths about the divine which lie beyond reason in the realm of revelation, such truths as divinity being personal, the Trinity, the incarnation, the resurrection, providence, etc. Such teachings, though not contrary to reason, cannot be established by reason, but reach us through revelation, embodied in the holy scriptures and in the consistent tradition and teaching of the Church. This is the realm of faith, where although faith does require an intellectual act of assent — we have got to make a decision for God and we make it using our intellectual gifts to the best of our ability — something more than the intellect is required. This something more is the maintenance of that decision, that act of assent, after it has been made. Faith requires faithfulness if it is to last, and faithfulness is something which we sustain by committing ourselves to belief in the midst of all the different experiences, both good and bad, which we go through in daily life. Faithfulness is grounded in the commitment to belief, the will to persevere, and this is in the end the test of whether our act of assent to faith in God is sincere. Our faith in God is tested by the extent to which we trust him and his providence.

It is at this point that we realize that philosophy and revelation alike depend upon the prevenient grace of God, which both enables us to think intelligently in the first place and then secondly brings us the gift of faith to fulfil the intimations of divinity outlined by reason prior to acceptance of the revealed truths found in the Church and in holy scripture.

Thirdly, St Thomas tackles the issue of knowledge. How do we know anything at all? What is the means of gaining knowledge and how reliable is the knowledge we gain? First, his conviction that the universe has being means that there is an objective world outside us and beyond us to be explored. Our knowledge is not simply a series of internal impressions synthesized within the mind to produce a series of solely subjective pieces of information. There is real impact from outside that provides the data from which knowledge is accumulated. What he is presenting is, in modern terms, a scientific approach to the universe.

Similarly, because God is also being, though this time non-contingent being, our knowledge of him is not simply a series of internal impressions synthesized within the mind to produce a series of solely subjective pieces of information; but, rather, his grace provides a real impact from outside ourselves providing the believer with data from which he grows in knowledge of God.

If we accept that this is so, then the matter resolves itself into the issue of how we receive the data from outside, whether it be from God or from his creation. There must be an appropriate means of doing so that is able to respond suitably to the impact from outside. It would be of no use trying to use an inappropriate 'receiver' to collect data to which it cannot relate. For example, an astronomer would not use a radio telescope to scan space for evidence of ultra-violet radiation, nor would a mother put in ear plugs and rely on her eyes if she wished to hear if her baby were crying. There is a vital likeness, an affinity between what is known and the means of knowing it.

This approach to knowledge will be explored in more detail in the next chapter. Suffice to say at this stage that, because man is a physical being as well as an intellectual being, and because the creation is largely physical, the development of knowledge begins at the physical interface between man and his environment. That is to say, we begin to explore the world around us through our five senses of sight, hearing, touch, taste and smell, and that understanding the sensations which are relayed to us — significantly called 'making sense' of our surroundings — is an intellectual process which depends in the first place upon reliable data received through the sense organs of the eyes, ears, skin, tongue and nose.

However, these sense organs only provide data at one level. Man is not solely physical. He also has intellectual powers — indeed it is precisely here that his human nature resides — and therefore there has to be intellectual means of building upon the information provided through the sense organs. Physical sense perception cannot by itself develop intellectual knowledge, and other ways are required which are able to seek such knowledge.

There must be a different set of 'receivers'. These 'receivers' are the intellectual powers of man which St John calls the faculties of understanding, memory and will. These will be explored in more detail in the next chapter.

Nevertheless, it is important to point out at this stage that this principle of an affinity between the means of knowing and what is known has an important consequence in our consideration of the way the grace of God works in our lives, which needs to be examined in some detail before we move on to the consideration of the theological basis of St John's spirituality.

Different people are at different stages in their pilgrimage of faith and yet all are sustained in that pilgrimage by the grace of God. Even if this pilgrimage is not yet characterized by the quality of faith, even so the grace of God in creation sustains each person in that condition, since existence itself is due to him. Our experience of God changes as we change; and, vice versa, as we change our experience of God changes. His influence in our lives is appropriate to what we can comprehend and receive beneficially. His grace must operate in us in such a way that we can receive it and use it.

So, it follows that God's grace does not operate in a blanket way, covering all things equally and indiscriminately, but rather that God causes his grace to operate in creation, including ourselves, in accordance with our nature. As we progress, and our human nature changes more and more into the likeness of Christ, so the working of God's grace changes to meet our new requirements. At each and every stage, his grace is sufficient for us, but that sufficiency is tailor-made at each stage to meet the particular requirements of that stage in our life. To know the grace of God requires that the grace of God is received by each of us in the manner in which our progress along the mystic way has prepared us to receive it. There is an implied warning here not to run before we can walk, but there is also the implied judgement that of those to whom much is given, much will be required. To turn backwards on the mystic path is as dangerous as to run headlong along it. God's grace is transforming our nature in order to allow us to receive further assistance along the path to union with God, and it is our task to be responsive to his gracious initiative.

All these factors play a central part in the spirituality of St John and provide him with the following theological basis for his mystical teaching.

First St John declares roundly, 'All the being of creation... compared with the infinite Being of God, is nothing. Therefore, the soul that sets its affection on the being of creation is likewise nothing in the eyes of God,... for, love makes equality and similitude, and even sets the lover below the object of his love. And therefore such a soul will in no wise be able to attain to union with the infinite Being of God' (*As.* I, 4, 4). In accordance with the Christian understanding of creation, there is presented here a radical break between the uncreated, infinite, non-contingent being of God and the created, finite, contingent being of all else. Therefore anyone who aspires to attain union with God must set his heart on the being of God and not be drawn aside by love of created things. The choice lies between a union of love within creation and a union of love with God. This is not to be misunderstood to mean that those who set their affections upon creation are without value in the eyes of God. The doctrine of creation in itself gives all things value in God's eyes, and that value is reinforced by the saving work of Christ. Rather, St John is comparing finite being with infinite being and making the point that it is inappropriate to become attached to what is finite, and therefore by comparison with the infinite is nothing, when seeking to attain union with the infinite God. He quotes the examples of created beauty, compared with the infinite beauty of God, as inadequate and unattractive, even deformed, and of the goodness of created things, compared with the infinite goodness of God, as potentially evil and wicked, since only God is in himself good.

So, St John writes, 'Favour is deceitful and beauty is vain. And thus the soul that is affectioned to the beauty of any creature is as the height of deformity in the eyes of God. And therefore this soul that is deformed will be unable to become transformed in beauty, which is God, since deformity cannot attain to beauty.... Thus it cannot be capable of the infinite grace and loveliness of God, for that which has no grace is far removed from that which is infinitely gracious' (*As.*I, 4, 4).

Similarly, St John insists that all human ability and knowledge are ignorance compared with the infinite wisdom of God. Therefore they are not appropriate means of seeking union with God (*As*.I, 4, 5). We can think about the world we live in and discover through knowledge a great deal about it; we can use our reason to think about God and his ways with mankind; but neither will bring us to union with God. The most they can do is to provide a start for those of intellectual ability, a start which has to be left behind as progress is made towards union with God. St John writes, 'In order to come to union with the wisdom of God, the soul has to proceed rather by unknowing than by knowing' (*As*.I, 4, 5). Again, the fact that the Christian life is lived 'in Christ' means that St John is making a comparison between the finite limits of the human mind to understand God's nature, and the wisdom of God himself which is infinite, and therefore, by definition, surpasses human understanding. He is not saying that it is impossible to know God, but that what can be known intellectually cannot grasp the wisdom of God in its entirety without remainder. God remains always 'incomprehensible', beyond our intellectual grasp, even though Jesus, the wisdom of God incarnate, has revealed God to us in himself. It is a revelation which in no way exhausts or limits the infinite nature of God.

Thirdly, St John rejects the pursuit of worldly desires as a means to union with God. If we become attached to the pursuit of power and high office, then we shall be enslaved by them and be regarded in God's eyes as such. If we become attached to our desires for freedom of action for wealth and for pleasure, then we shall be captured by those desires and enslaved by them, reducing ourselves in the sight of God to the level of a prisoner. Loving power and position, the indulgence of human pleasure and satisfaction, lowers our horizon to the level of these things, making us lose sight of the union which counts, namely, union with the liberty of God as a son of God, giving us true freedom, and with the glory of God which transforms us into the likeness of Christ, in whom dwell all the true riches, the riches of God's grace.

So St John writes, 'The soul that is enamoured of prelacy (i.e. any kind of preferential position). . . . and longs for liberty of desire, is considered and treated in the sight of God, not as a son, but as a base slave.... therefore such a soul will be unable to attain to that true liberty of spirit which is encompassed in his divine union' (*As.*I, 4,6). Also, 'all the delights and pleasures of the will in all the things of the world, in comparison with all those delights which are God, are supreme affliction, torment and bitterness. And thus he that sets his heart upon them... will be unable to attain to the delights of the embrace of union with God.... All the wealth and glory of all creatures, in comparison with the wealth which is God, is supremely poverty and wretchedness. Thus the soul that loves and possesses creature wealth is supremely poor and wretched in the sight of God, and for this reason will be unable to attain to that wealth and glory which is the state of transformation in God' (*As.*I, 4, 7). Yet again, the fact that St John's faith is centred in Christ makes it clear that he is reminding his readers that they need the same attitude as Jesus who, as Son of man, 'came not to be served but to serve and to give his life as a ransom for many'. This is the required approach which leads to the transformation of those who seek union with God from 'one degree of glory to another' into the likeness of Christ.

What St John is emphasizing is really very simple and obvious, but difficult to achieve. He is making it very clear that any progress to union with God can only be made by taking appropriate steps to achieve the goal. Inappropriate steps only hinder progress or worse, lead us off the right path down roads which lead to the distortion and ultimately the destruction of the spiritual life. 'Blessed are the pure in heart, for they shall see God.' Purity of heart means singleness of purpose, and nothing of lasting value is achieved unless we have that one overriding intention which is the guiding influence for the whole of our life.

Because nothing in creation can equal God in importance, the person who seeks union with God will seek to love God above all else. Even the idea of two loves — love for God and love for other things — cannot be sustained, let alone loving anything else without God, as a way of progressing to union with God. Any love for other things must be held within love for God, so that any attachment which love brings is attachment to God, and not to things in themselves, outside love for God. In practice, this means being prepared to place second in our lives all loves

33

except love for God, to cut down to size, or if needs be reject, any other love which threatens to undermine or compromise our love for God, and to use self-denial and repentance where appropriate, as means of purifying our affections if other attachments get in the way of our attachment to God, believing that such a sacrifice will be blessed with a new understanding of God and a new love for God as the fruits of a growing attachment to him. St Bernard in his treatise *On loving God* sets out four stages of love which illustrate St John's point. These are:

> loving oneself for one's own sake,
> loving God for one's own sake,
> loving God for God's sake,
> loving oneself for God's sake.

Here the progression from selfish to selfless love is clearly set out, in which love for God gradually takes over control of our life so that in the end all is loved for God's sake. St Bernard points out that very few people reach the fourth stage; it is the equivalent of St John's understanding of union with God.

The next theological point which has a vital practical application to progress towards union is the clear distinction between faith and reason, already set out above. Because reason cannot carry us all the way to understanding God, it cannot bring us to union with God. The very nature of God is 'other' than us, beyond our intellectual grasp, incomprehensible, and therefore to attain to union with God requires that we be prepared 'to proceed rather by unknowing than by knowing' (*As.*I, 4, 5). 'Faith our outward sense befriending, makes the inward vision clear', wrote St Thomas Aquinas. But this clearness produced by faith is not the clarity of intellectual insight, rather it is the conviction held by faith that union with God is possible. Because reason cannot lead us all the way to God, the path to union must be trod by faith, in a 'dark night' where reason is unable to penetrate because it is blind in the dark. The concept of the path to union as 'night' is a fundamental insight in St John's writings. By it he does not mean that occasionally our spiritual journey is darkened by aridity, suffering or sin, and that any respite from these produces light. This is not his meaning. The 'dark night of the soul' is a permanent state which may be intensified by human weakness and suffering, but in reality exists because of

34

the nature of God, not the afflictions of man. Faith is not reason; if we wish to progress beyond the knowledge supplied by our senses and analyzed by our intellectual faculties, then we must detach ourselves from them, leaving them behind, in order to journey towards union with God. 'In order for the understanding to be prepared for this divine union, it must be pure and void from all that pertains to sense, and detached and freed from all that can clearly be perceived by the understanding profoundly hushed and put to silence, and leaning upon faith, which alone is the proximate and proportionate means whereby the soul is united with God; for such is the likeness between itself and God that there is no other difference, save that which exists between seeing God and believing in him' (*As.*II, 9, 1). The fact that God is uncreated, infinite being means that there is not enough likeness between him and our created, finite being to enable the intellectual insights, gathered by reason from the senses, to see the way to union. We must abandon the inadequate resources of reason in favour of the darkness of faith. The advantage that faith has over reason is that it provides 'the proximate and proportionate means' to union, because union with God is based, not on ability on our part to grasp him intellectually, but on belief that he is. Our goal lies beyond the highest thing that can be known or experienced; therefore we must pass beyond everything into unknowing. To reach that goal we exercise our faith. 'As God is infinite, so faith sets him before us as infinite; and as he is Three and One, it sets him before us as Three and One; and as God is darkness to our understanding, even so does faith likewise blind and dazzle our understanding. And thus, by this means alone, God manifests himself to the soul in divine light, which passes all understanding. And therefore, the greater is the faith of the soul, the more completely is it united with God .... He that will be united with God .... must walk by faith in his journey to him, the understanding being blind and in darkness, walking in faith alone' (*As.*II, 9, 1).

St John sums up his use of the term 'night' as follows. 'There are three reasons for which this journey made by the soul to union with God is called night. The first has to do with the point from which the soul goes forth, for it has gradually to deprive itself of desire for all worldly things which it possessed,

35

by denying them to itself; the which denial and deprivation are, as it were, night to all the senses of man. The second reason has to do with the mean (manner), or the road along which the soul must travel to this union — that is, faith, which is likewise as dark as night to the understanding. The third has to do with the point to which it travels — namely God, who, equally, is dark night to the soul in this life. These three nights must pass through the soul — or rather, the soul must pass through them — in order that it may come to divine union with God' (*As.*I, 2, 1). We have looked at the second and third reasons in some detail; the first, 'to do with the point from which the soul goes forth' will be considered at length later.

The last theological point to be applied to St John's analysis of the path to union is the truth that God's grace operates in created things in accordance with their nature. Since the graciousness of God lies in the fact that he is leading us forward, step by step, to union with him, loving us even more than we love him, guiding our feet along the right path for our good, not doing violence to us or asking us to go beyond what he knows we are capable of at any particular moment, it follows that the process of raising us to union through the influence of the grace of God upon us progresses with an order and harmony which accords with the changes that have been wrought in us so far. God starts the work of leading us to union at the level of sense knowledge and gradually leads the soul to his spiritual wisdom which is beyond sense. The process is a natural chain, each movement linked into the next. God brings us to perfection according to the way of our human nature. That nature is not abused or put aside, but transformed. 'Man fully alive is the glory of God' (St Irenaeus). God wants us to be united with him as complete human beings, not as creatures who have denied or tried to cast off their humanity. We are not called to reject our nature, which is God-given, but to deny our sins which are barriers to union. In St Bernard's terms to love oneself for God's sake is the highest operation of God's grace in the soul, and it is achieved by a step-by-step development of our human nature into a centring of life upon God. Thus, it is possible to outline a way of spiritual progress which is in principle open to all human beings, a true Christian humanism in which the value and integrity of every person is affirmed in a vision of man which has as its purpose and goal the union of man, transformed and perfected, with God, the creator and redeemer of the universe.

However, from the seventeenth century onwards, philosophers began to explore the possibility of a world-view without God, and the rise of utilitarian and moral philosophies during the Enlightenment led to a decline in philosophies of ontology, resulting in a loss of a sense of being as the basis for constructing a comprehensive understanding of the world and of man. This decline was paralleled in theology by a decline in the influence of Thomism. Twentieth century existentialism and logical positivism, the heirs of the Enlightenment, have redrawn the area under consideration by philosophers. They have withdrawn from the great task of seeking the meaning of existence into the reduced arena of the absurd and the non-sense. Such philosophies cannot carry the concept of God and therefore are of no use in seeking to relate man to God — indeed, they would specifically deny such a task as being proper to them. The fact that these movements in philosophy have moved away from ontology in no way makes them necessarily a true or beneficial progression of thought in the perennial task of placing man in his environment, and those who have faith in the God and Father of Our Lord Jesus Christ may justifiably react against the reduction of man and his world to the meagre dimension permitted by some modern philosophers. We may well play Hamlet to their Horatio. The great strength of Thomism is that it neither plays down human nature as irrational or bestial, nor plays up human nature as intellectual or spiritual, but rather, sets us firmly in the context of a solid world of real things in which God acts to achieve relationship without either obliterating the individual or distorting his nature. Whatever the philosophical weaknesses of Thomism in detail, its strength lies in its hard-headed realism as to the human condition and the human potential, and as such it remains a very useful vehicle for expounding the path to union with God.

4. Things Human

In the last chapter, entitled 'Things Divine', we examined St John's theology in order to understand how the nature of God defines the manner of our progress to union with him. That understanding of the nature of God cannot be kept entirely separate from a parallel exploration of the nature of man. We have already seen how the Thomist theory of knowledge and the relationship between reason and faith interact, rooted as they are in the two sources of knowledge, the sense world around us and divine revelation. This requires us to try to penetrate not only the mystery of God but also the mystery of man. The difference in the two attempts is that one, the attempt to penetrate the divine nature, is recognized from the start as only a limited expedition into the unknown and unknowable, whereas the other, the attempt to penetrate human nature, is in principle capable of much fuller and more exhaustive exploration. We are created and finite, and therefore open to scientific examination. In this chapter, we shall be pursuing precisely this task; we shall be looking at 'things human', the psychological basis for St John's writings.

The first point to make is that, like his theology, St John's psychology is rooted in Thomism, under the general heading of 'faculty psychology' which refers to the idea of there being 'faculties' of the soul. But unlike Thomist theology, the psychology which stands in that same general tradition does not have such a clear-cut and universally accepted terminology. The general ideas are similar but each theologian develops his own psychological language. St John is no exception. He is both within the Thomist tradition and an original thinker.

However, because the psychological model used by St John is very different from that used in the twentieth century by Freud and his successors, it is necessary to put on one side, as far as possible, the current terminology and the presuppositions behind it, and remember that we are dealing with a pre-Freudian analysis of the human psyche. Many modern psychological terms such as emotion, mind, the unconscious, personality and so on, find virtually no place in St John's vocabulary. Also, just to complicate matters further, other terms, with which we are familiar, of which just two examples are imagination and memory, are used by St John but do not mean to him what they currently mean to us. St John's psychological language is attempting to describe human experience and it is at that level — the level of experience — that we should seek to follow his thought. Then his terminology will make sense, because it will relate to ourselves and our own experience of our environment. We may find that some of his language can translate into modern psychological terms, but on the whole it is probably more advantageous to take it as a viable way of describing what it means to be human, independently of other thought patterns on the same subject. What we are looking at is the structure and working of the soul as expounded by the medieval schoolmen and their successors, taken over and developed in a striking and original way by one of the greatest exponents of the mystic way.

Of course, the Thomist theory of knowledge, and its distinction between faith and reason, are not the only incentives for examining human psychology. There is in addition the directly theological incentive arising from the fact already developed that God moves all things according to their nature. To seek to understand the soul is not only to advance in understanding ourselves, but, even more important, to understand how God's grace can act upon the soul at various levels and how the soul in its different ways can respond effectively to and derive most benefit from the influence of divine grace upon it. Self-understanding is integral to progress along the way to union with God.

St John's view of our human nature is that we are tripartite, that is to say, for the sake of analysis we can be seen as a three-fold being. However, he does not mean by this that in day-to-day life we fall into three parts, or that in reality we can be taken to pieces. He emphasizes that we are each of us a single person, that we have an ontological continuity of body and soul. In modern terms, St John would agree that we are psychosomatic.

The basis of our human nature is the body. St John does not analyse the body as such, but that does not mean that he despises it or regards it as anything other than good. Indeed his emphasis is upon our nature as being one single entity. Talking of the dark night of the spirit, he refers to this point and the communication which there is between the different parts of our nature (*Dk.Nt.* II, 1,1).

The way the body and soul relate is one of mutual need and interdependence. We are not in the Platonic world of the good soul imprisoned in an evil body. Quite the opposite. The soul is the body's governing principle, like the rudder of a ship. The body needs the soul to give it direction and order. But in return, the soul depends on the body for its knowledge of the world around it, because of the principle that all knowledge starts from sense-information through the five sense organs of the body. The soul governs the body, but the soul depends upon the body for information through its sense organs of the eyes, ears, nose, tongue, skin. Both must work in harmony, relying on each other, if the person is to flourish.

The soul and its development as the person progresses towards union with God is St John's major concern and therefore we find that his analysis of the soul is both subtle and sophisticated. Rather than attempt to define what the word means at this stage, it is probably better to consider St John's analysis of the soul and attempt a definition at the end.

St John describes the soul as having two parts or, perhaps better, two levels of operation. '(This night) is likewise darker (in its second part) than the first part, for this belongs to the lower part of man, which is the sensual (sensitive) part.... This second part, which is of faith, belongs to the higher part of man, which is the rational part, and, in consequence, more interior and more obscure' (*As.*II, 2, 2).

The lower level or part is called the animal soul or sometimes the sensitive part. This level of the soul is where it relates directly to the body, through the senses. These senses are themselves of two sorts. First, there are the five 'exterior corporeal senses', that is to say, our senses of sight, hearing, taste, smell and touch. Each of these exterior corporeal senses in the animal soul corresponds to a sensory organ of the body. Thus, the sense of sight in the soul relates to the eye of the body, the sense of hearing in the soul to the ear. St John distinguishes between the sensory organ and the sense itself because it is possible to have one without the other, e.g. those who are deaf have ears but not hearing. Nevertheless, it is clear that the animal soul is intimately allied to the sense organs, through the exterior corporeal senses, a fact substantiated in our own time by our greater understanding of the working of the nervous system. This is not to say that had St John our present knowledge of the nervous system he would have included that and the brain in the soul; rather our present knowledge shows us more minutely than was possible for him to analyse just how intimately the body and the animal soul are placed.

But the animal soul does not possess solely exterior corporeal senses. It also possesses two 'interior corporeal senses' called imagination and fancy. Of these two, the former is by far the more important and needs to be considered in detail. The use of the term, 'imagination', strikes a modern note which must be disregarded. We are not dealing with the modern idea of imagination at all, or its derivatives such as imaginary, meaning not real or not realistic. Rather the faculty of the soul covered by the imagination, as used by St John, is capable of both the modern meaning and the process of putting together sense experience into realistic patterns. Thus the imagination is the power of the animal soul to see a piece of stone and to see a man and then imagine a statue of the man carved out of the stone — precisely the process that Michelangelo used when choosing his 'hunks of meat' in the marble quarries of Carrara.

It may seem strange that St John places the faculty of imagination in the animal soul, but he does so because of the Thomist theory of knowledge. Because all our knowledge is based, first of all, upon our sense perception, it follows that the imagination can only work on such things as fall within our perceptual experience. The imagination is an internal sense, equivalent to one of the external senses, which simply combines the external experience in different configurations. These configurations need not be in touch with the world outside the body — some are, and some are not — but all of them are the product of perceptual experience, and perceptual experience alone. There is nothing in itself rational in this — the harnessing of the imagination to the dictates of reason is a function of the next level of the soul's operation; rather we have here a mechanical ability which is limited by the material supplied to it by the five exterior corporeal senses. Thus, for example, we can imagine a man with a horse's head, or a blue lemon, for although such things do not exist their components do; but we cannot imagine a two-sided triangle or a colour not derived from the constituents of the rainbow because they fall outside our perceptual experience. This makes the imagination essentially an interior sense perceiving what is stored up in the soul, analogous to the exterior senses perceiving the material things of the world around us. Thus, when St John uses the word 'imaginary' he does not necessarily mean unreal, but rather uses it precisely as an adjective referring strictly to its parent noun, imagination, with its reference to the making of images out of sense experience. Thus St John writes, 'In this second book, the first thing that has now to be treated is the interior bodily sense — namely, the imagination and the fancy...two interior bodily senses...which subserve each other in due order. For the one sense reasons, as it were, by imagining, and the other forms the imagination, or that which is imagined, by making use of the fancy. For our purpose the discussion of the one is equivalent to that of the other, and, for this reason, when we name them both, we are to be understood as speaking of either.... All the things, then, that these senses can receive and fashion are known as imaginations and fancies, which are forms that are represented to these senses by bodily figures and images. This can happen in two ways...one way is supernatural...the other way is natural...thus to these two faculties belongs meditation, which is a discursive action wrought by means of images, forms and figures that are produced and imagined by the said senses, as when we imagine Christ crucified, or bound to the column, or at another of the stations (of the Cross); or when we imagine God seated upon a throne with great majesty; or when we consider or imagine glory to be like a most beauteous light etc.; or when we imagine all kinds of other things, whether divine or human' (*As*.II, 12, 2-3). It is clear from this that the second interior corporeal sense, the fancy, is simply the ability to stabilize or hold an image from the imagination, so that it can be considered at length. As such, it relates to the common parlance of taking a fancy to something or someone, e.g. I fancy an ice cream. Here is a sustained image held in anticipation of the pleasure that the ice cream will bring.

We are now in a position to consider the second level of operation in the soul. The sensitive part receives information through the sense organs and, by means of its five exterior corporeal senses and two interior corporeal senses, prepares the material for further assessment. This further assessment occurs at the second level of operation which St John calls the higher part of the soul. This higher part is the place of the rational or spiritual faculties, which St John describes as three in number — the memory, the understanding and the will. One obvious difference between St John's terminology is that we confine the use of 'rational' and 'intellectual' to our ability to understand, whereas St John sees all these faculties as 'intellectual faculties', that is to say, capable of reason. He also calls them 'spiritual faculties', so that he sometimes calls this higher part of the soul not only the rational soul, but also at times, the spirit.

Thus, we can see that the whole person is tripartite; divided for purposes of analysis into body and soul, with the soul in turn divided into a lower, sensitive part and a higher part, the spirit. As with all technical language, its meaning derives from the use made of it by the technician. Here St John is not using this three-fold structure in the same way as other writers have used 'trinities' to describe the person. St Paul's division of the person into body, soul and spirit, and the common Stoic division into body, soul and mind are not the same divisions as the division of the person by St John into body, sensitive part and spirit. For him, the sensitive part and the spirit are both parts of the one soul, not entities in themselves, independent of each other.

It is worth noticing also in passing that St John uses the term 'faculty' in two ways, referring to the 'sensible faculties', which are the powers of sight, hearing, smell, taste and touch and the 'spiritual faculties' of memory, understanding and will. Quite often he does not qualify the word with its appropriate adjective, and those reading his works should take care to check the context in which the word is used until they are familiar with his use of language.

But in all this analysis of the person into parts, it must remain our overriding concern to retain our grasp on the unity of the person, that we are psychosomatic, operating out of one consciousness, one self-awareness. Our various functions and faculties reciprocate, each relating intimately and subtly with the others, making for responses, attitudes and actions that are integrated, and expressive of ourselves and our individuality.

What are the functions of the memory, the understanding and the will? The memory is the faculty of the spirit which works in close co-operation with the imagination and the exterior corporeal senses. Its task is to reduce these sense impressions to order and to store them so that they can be recalled. Thus, St John calls the memory 'an archive and storehouse....wherein are received all forms and images that can be understood; and thus the soul has them within itself as it were a mirror, having received them by means of the five senses, or, as we say, supernaturally; and thus (the memory) presents them to the understanding' (As.II, 16, 2). But this is not the limit to the power of memory — it is far more than a recording machine. Not only does it recall past experience; it also has the equally important function of looking forward to the future. The memory is the source of our anticipation. This may seem rather odd, since our own perception of memory is concerned with past events. In this respect we are different from, say, the ancient Greeks, for whom the idea of remembering — anamnesis — meant bringing the past into the present so that remembering means bringing forward events, not looking back on them. Here is the New Testament idea of the Eucharist as a remembering of the sacrifice of Christ. St John's idea of memory is different again — and a salient example of the care we have to take with the use of words if we are not to be led astray — in that he perceives that any forward thinking that we do is done upon the evidence of material received in the past. We anticipate the future on the basis of evidence we already possess. Again we may instinctively feel that such anticipation should belong to the imagination, but we must remember that to anticipate the future is a rational activity based on assessment of the material presented — our predictions should be carefully thought through and formulated from the evidence before us. Therefore, it is in the memory, which is a rational faculty, that such assessment occurs, not in the imagination which has no rationality. It is because the memory brings order and shape to the sense data received from the animal soul that it is able to prepare us to consider rationally what lies ahead.

The understanding is a difficult faculty to appreciate because its function overlaps with, but is not identical to, the modern psychological term 'intellect'. All three faculties of the spirit are rational, but the understanding is distinguished from the memory and the will by its ability to comprehend. It is the seat of logical ratiocination, the faculty that 'thinks things through'. But we cannot 'think things through' without being presented with the 'things' to be 'thought through' in the first place. Therefore discourse within the mind requires the use of the memory working in harmony with the understanding. Theirs is an intimate collaboration in which the understanding receives the material from the senses of the animal soul, together with and through the memory, and by exercising its power to comprehend, produces knowledge. This knowledge — scientific information, if you like, of the world around us — is then stored in the memory for recall as required. Apart from certain supernatural communications, which we shall discuss later, the limits of the knowledge available to the understanding are drawn by the sense impressions received from the senses, exterior and interior, plus the use of logical inference derived from the sense information received. The dependence of the understanding upon the sense information received is the source of another of the bonds between the spirit and the animal soul in which the former depends upon the latter, just as the animal soul in turn depends upon the bodily organs for its sense perception in the first place. The tongue tastes some food and transmits an image to the sense of taste; this sense perceives the image and transmits its perception of it to the memory and the understanding; the understanding comprehends the knowledge it is being given, assimilates and stores it in the memory.

The third faculty of the spirit is the will. Here we are considering the power of the spirit which makes us essentially human. For St John, human acts as such differ from all other acts of animals and from the actions of inanimate creatures precisely in that they are of the will. In principle, the will is the arbiter and governor of the whole personality, gathering up and directing the powers of the soul. The point here is that whereas all else in creation is subject to the law of cause and effect, human beings are able to break out of that process by rational thought and action. We are endowed with free will, able to make free choices of our own volition. Or at least ideally this is so. In practice, the ideal is rarely the case. Other considerations complicate the issue. First, certain acts which we do are not distinctively human, e.g. reflex reactions. Nor is the will master in its own house. Sin, and its consequences, mean that the curse of the old Adam plays havoc with the scope for freedom held by the will. It should be the governing principle in our lives, but the influence of natural desires and natural passions (see below) undermine the strength of the will to choose rightly. But ideally, the business of the will, aided by the knowledge gained by the understanding and assimilated by the memory, is to govern the passions and to hold in check the natural appetites, in order to co-ordinate and direct the whole attitude and activity of the complete person. Again, we see here a dependence already found in the understanding and the memory. The will cannot be independent either of the animal soul or of the body. They impose limits upon its action; it can only move in accordance with the data they transmit to it. Indeed, without the flow of data from the senses, the will would remain permanently unactivated and inactive. Without the body and the animal soul, the will would have no material to act upon and no way of gaining self-consciousness. Indeed, the will is further limited in its decision-making by the limitations placed upon it by the understanding. Even though the will may be able to direct our attention towards a particular object, any further action by the will involving a decision about the object and our reaction to it is dependent upon the rational assessment of the object by the understanding. We all know the paralysis of the will that occurs when we are suddenly confronted with a new experience which the understanding cannot adequately assess.

Thus, for St John the work of the soul is to relate human beings to their environment by building up from the experience of the sense organs of the body a comprehensive stock of knowledge upon which to take action. The fact that the process requires bringing order and harmony to the data provided by the environment means that the soul needs to have natural powers over and above the simple ability to receive sense stimulation. This in turn requires the analysis of the soul to divide it into two parts — the animal soul, or sensitive part, and the rational soul, or spirit; but such a schematic division must not blind us to the greater truth that the parts work together naturally as a whole, and awareness of our own souls is not normally in the form of the dissection presented here. Rather, we simply respond to the sensations received by the body directly so that the steps in the process are not discerned. However, since progress towards union with God entails movement within the soul, St John, as a physician of the soul, must understand its structure in order to relate the reader to the ways in which the grace of God operates within the soul, leading it to union.

To grasp the import of this analysis of the soul it is useful to remind ourselves of the goal we are pursuing. God's grace is the means to an end, and it is vital to understand what that end is in order to make best use of the means provided. St John, following St Thomas Aquinas, describes that union with God which is our goal as 'a linking and conjoining of two things, which though united, are still different'. This definition of union is expressly designed to maintain the nature of each of the two things, because to do otherwise would not be to describe union but identity or absorption. Thus St John rules out any pantheistic, Gnostic or Hindu interpretation of union with God in favour of the conviction that union of the soul with God will be a linking and conjoining of the soul with God and of God with the soul, in such a way that the soul is still the soul and God is still God. This is, as we have seen already, the basis of all true Christian mysticism, and a truth which needs to be remembered over and over again because it maintains the personal character of our human nature even in the vision of God. The biblical understanding of our relationship with God as between two irreducible centres of personal consciousness and will is always at the heart of St John's teaching. Of course, when two things are united in this sense, the one which has the most power, virtue and activity will exercise the larger influence upon the other. Therefore we anticipate that in union God communicates his properties to the soul and deifies it to a greater or lesser degree, depending on the degree of union between the two; but this process is never to the destruction of our humanity, but always the transfiguration of our humanity from one degree of glory to another. St John never talks of the essential or ontological union of the soul with God because dependent, contingent, created being (the soul) cannot unite in essence with non-contingent, uncreated being (God); rather he is always talking of a union between the soul and God through the power of his grace developing within us the virtues of faith, hope and love and the gifts of the Holy Spirit. We can actively work for such a union by striving to co-operate with the grace of God in seeking these virtues and gifts and exercising them rightly, so that we will what God wills and reject what God rejects. It is because we have our part to play in this movement to union that St John develops his psychology. Faith, hope and love do not develop in the soul out of nothing, but relate to the faculties of the soul, each virtue transforming the soul into alignment with God's purposes and promoting union between the soul and its Creator (cf. *As.*II, 5, note 3). Furthermore, there is consolation in knowing that essential union with God is not possible. St John puts it thus: 'However lofty are the communications of a soul with God in this life, and the revelation of his presence, and however high and exalted is its knowledge of him, they are not God in his essence, nor have they aught to do with him. For in truth he is still hidden from the soul, and it ever beseems the soul, amid all these grandeurs, to consider him as hidden.... If the soul should experience any great communication or knowledge of God, or any other feeling, it must not for that reason persuade itself that it possesses God more completely or is more deeply in God; nor that which it feels or understands is God in his essence, however profound such experiences may be; and if all these sensible and intelligible communications fail, it must not think that for that reason God is failing it. For in reality the one estate can give no assurance to a soul that it is in his grace, neither can the other, that it is without it' (*Sp.Cant.* I, 2). Let us return to the rational faculties of the spirit and apply these principles to them.

The memory, as the seat not only of our ability to reduce to order and store up our sense perceptions and knowledge gained by the understanding, but also of our power to anticipate the future, is seen by St John as the faculty upon which the grace of God moves to develop within us the virtue of hope. 'We shall proceed....with regard to the memory, drawing it out from its natural methods and limitations, and causing it to rise above itself — that is, above all clear knowledge and apprehensible possessions — to the supreme hope of God, who is incomprehensible' (*As.* III, 2, 3). Here in the memory lie remembered past acts of God's providence towards us and therefore the material upon which to look forward to union with God in hope. The way in which that looking forward can be assisted to fulfilment is to be considered later. Suffice to quote St John, 'The memory must...strip itself of all...forms and notions, that it may unite itself with God in hope. For all possession is contrary to hope, which as St Paul says, belongs to that which is not possessed. Wherefore, the more the memory dispossesses itself, the greater is its hope; and the more it has of hope, the more it has of union with God; for with respect to God, the more the soul hopes, the more it attains' (*As.* III, 7, 2).

The understanding, as the seat of knowledge, is seen by St John as the faculty upon which the grace of God moves to develop within us the virtue of faith. It is worth recalling at this point the distinction between faith and knowledge. Knowledge derives from sense perceptions and is a body of organized scientific information, whereas 'faith...is a habit of the soul, certain and obscure' (*As.* II, 3, 1). Therefore, 'All that...the understanding can receive and understand in this life is not, nor can it be, a proximate means to union with God' (*As.* II, 8, 4), because they are not appropriate means to achieve the desired end. Faith is the appropriate means because faith is grounded in revelation from God, and the understanding needs to be transformed by the virtue of faith in order to be united with God. This will involve darkness and emptiness, both because the light of faith is beyond the comprehension of the understanding and because the accumulated body of knowledge in the understanding is of no help on the journey. 'In order for the understanding to be prepared for this divine union, it must be pure and void of all that pertains to sense, and detached and freed from all that can clearly be perceived by the understanding, profoundly

49

hushed and put to silence, and leaning upon faith, which alone is the proximate and proportionate means whereby the soul is united with God; for such is the likeness between itself and God that there is no other difference, save that which exists between seeing God and believing in him. For, as God is infinite, so faith sets him before us as infinite; and as he is Three and One, it sets him before us as Three and One; and as God is darkness to our understanding, even so does faith likewise blind and dazzle our understanding. And thus, by this means alone, God manifests himself to the soul in divine light, which passes all understanding. And therefore, the greater is the faith of the soul, the more completely is it united with God.... That is, (man) must walk by faith in his journey to him, the understanding being blind and in darkness, walking with faith alone' (*As.* II, 9, 1).

The will, as the seat of overall control, decision-making and action, is seen by St John as the faculty upon which the grace of God moves to develop within us the virtue of love. The will of God is the alignment of our will to his. The content of God's will is summed up in love, for 'God is love'. Therefore, the human will is called to respond with love to love. Faith and hope by themselves cannot carry us to full union with God — full union is a union of love. Thus St John writes, 'We should have accomplished nothing by the purgation of the understanding in order to ground it in the virtue of faith, and by the purgation of the memory in order to ground it in hope, if we purged not the will also according to the third virtue, which is charity, whereby the works that are done in faith live and have great merit and without it are of no worth.... I find no more fitting authority than that which is written in the sixth chapter of Deuteronomy, where Moses says: "Thou shalt love the Lord thy God with all thy heart and with all thy soul and with all thy strength" (*As.* III, 16, 1). If this love causes an emptiness in the will then it does so because 'it obliges us to love God above...all (else); which cannot be unless we withdraw our affection from them all in order to set it wholly upon God' (*As.* II, 6, 4). St John quotes our Lord's saying, 'Unless a man renounces all that he has, he cannot be my disciple.'

Thus we are presented with an active programme of seeking to move forward through co-operation with God's grace, by developing as of first importance a union of faith, hope and love in the understanding, memory and will respectively. But this is not the whole of the story either from the point of view of further development along the way in passive states of union, or with respect to other considerations which come into play before a union of faith, hope and love is achieved. We must return to the animal soul and consider in further detail some of the psychological forces at work there which we ignore at our peril.

We need to consider what St John means when he refers to the passions and the affections. The passions are movements in the animal soul which arise under the influence of sense experience and cause us to react in particular ways. They are natural and involuntary acts and they are spontaneous inclinations arising out of the animal soul and have no rationality about them. However, if these passions are accepted by the spirit then they are rationalized and become known as the affections. We have here the same distinction as exists between the exterior and interior corporeal senses of the animal soul and the intellectual faculties of the spirit. Thus a passion received and accepted by the spirit is diffused into the memory and understanding to become a basis of activity by the will, that is to say, an influence upon the will in its decision-making, thus affecting the ability of the will to be the master of its own house. A passion thus accepted by the spirit is known as an affection, and in particular, an affection of the will.

Together, the passions and affections of the soul constitute what we would call the emotions. In themselves, they are morally neutral, so that their influence can be good or bad, so that they develop as virtues or vices depending on how the will acts upon them.

St John describes the passions and affections under four headings: joy, hope, grief and fear. The names of the first two are surprising, perhaps even shocking, referring as they usually do to two of the great Christian virtues, but the connotations put upon these words in the context of discussing the passions is quite different. Again, grasping the saint's terminology requires a careful consideration of the context.

These four passions relate to one another thus: joy is simply unreasoning animal delight in a basic, animal pleasure; hope is the anticipating of repeating that pleasure again; grief is the involuntary misery which follows from being hurt or denied pleasure; fear is the anticipation of such hurt or deprivation. So, joy and hope are positive passions; grief and fear are their negative counterparts. To give an example, we may enjoy playing football; we may hope to enjoy the game next week; we may become depressed when the coach tells us he has dropped us from the team; we may fear that we have lost our place in the team permanently. This gamut of reactions is morally neutral. What we do with them is all important. We may develop them into vices if they get out of hand, or, if the will is able to restrain them and direct them in good directions they become the source of all virtues.

St John has harsh words to say about the desires set up in the soul by the passions and affections, when they are not under the control of the will. 'The desires weary and fatigue the soul; for they are like restless and discontented children, who are ever demanding this or that from their mother, and are never satisfied' (*As.* I, 6, 6). 'Fire goes down when the wood is consumed, but desire, though it increases when the fuel is added to it, decreases not correspondingly when the fuel is consumed; on the contrary, instead of going down, as does the fire when its fuel is consumed, it fails from weariness, for its hunger is increased and its food diminished' (*As.* I, 6, 7). '(Another) evil which the desires cause the soul is in their tormenting and afflicting of it, after the manner of one who is in torment through being bound with cords from which he has no relief until he be freed.... The more intense is the desire, the greater is the torment which it causes to the soul. So that the torment increases with the desire; and the greater are the desires which possess the soul, the greater its torments' (*As.* I, 7, 1-2). 'The third evil that the desires cause in the soul is that they blind and darken it.... The soul is darkened in the understanding, it is stultified also in the will, and the memory becomes dull and disordered' (*As.* I, 8, 1-2). 'The fourth evil which the desires cause in the soul is that they stain and defile it.... This harm, and more, is done to the beauty of the soul by its unruly desires for the things of this world.... Any desire, although it be for but the smallest imperfection, stains and defiles the soul' (*As.* I, 9, 1-7). 'The fifth way in which the desires harm the soul is by making it lukewarm and weak, so that it has no strength to follow after virtue and to persevere therein…. Thus the reason why many souls have no diligence and eagerness to gain virtue is, as a rule, that they have desires and affections which are not pure and are not fixed upon God' (*As.* I, 10, 1-4).

It is clear that St John takes our emotional life seriously and recognizes the sway that feelings have over the course of events.

However, it must be added that St John does not ask the impossible, nor does the path to union require of us what is inhuman. We need to remind ourselves again that progress towards union with God is to transfigure our humanity, not to destroy or disfigure it. Therefore he distinguishes between various levels of desire. First there are the involuntary passions which simply crop up from time to time — these cannot be avoided, they are an ordinary everyday part of life. For example, feeling hunger or sexual drive is part of being human. These are no impediment to progress along the path to union provided they do not become an obsession, that is, a fixed affection of the will. 'All desires are not equally hurtful, nor do they all equally embarrass the soul…for the natural desires hinder the soul little, or not at all, from attaining to union, when they are not consented to nor pass beyond the first movements (that is, all those wherein the rational will has had no part, whether at first or afterward); and to take away these — that is, to mortify them wholly in this life — is impossible. And these hinder not the soul in such a way as to prevent attainment to divine union, even though they be not, as I say, wholly mortified; for the natural man may well have them, and yet the soul may be quite free from them according to the rational spirit. For it will sometimes come to pass that the soul will be in full union of the prayer of quiet in the will, while these desires are actually dwelling in the sensual part of the soul, and the higher part, which is in prayer, will have nothing to do with them' (*As.* I, 11, 2).

The danger point comes when these desires pass over into the rational soul and become affections of the will. Once this happens habits are beginning to form, bonds are being made, attitudes are shaping up, which can drag us into imperfection and sin. To feel a natural desire rising spontaneously within the animal soul is one thing; to stabilize it into a desire to be pursued is another. So, St John writes, 'Voluntary desires, whether they be of...sin...or whether they be only of imperfections...must be driven away every one, and the soul must be free from them all, howsoever small they be, if it is to come to this complete union; And the reason is that the state of this divine union consists in the soul's total transformation, according to the will, in the will of God, so that there is nought in the soul that is contrary to the will of God, but that, in all and through all, its movement may be that of the will of God alone' (*As.* I, 11, 2). The important qualifying word here is 'voluntary', that is, of the will. The voluntary desires to which St John refers are the affections of the will, and it is they, when imperfect or sinful, which hinder progress towards union with God, that is 'the making of two wills into one — namely, into the will of God, which will of God is likewise the will of the soul' (*As.* I, 11, 3).

The process is very difficult to sustain. Indeed St John recognizes that it is rare for total freedom from sin or even imperfection to occur and therefore the reaching of total union is rare. 'Some habits of voluntary imperfections, which are never completely conquered, prevent not only the attainment of divine union, but also progress in perfection' (*As.* I, 11, 3). Such imperfections (let alone sins) are so easy to accept that we may not even fully realize how attached to them we are, let alone how damaging they can be to the soul's progress. '(Such) habitual imperfections are, for example, a common custom of much speaking, or some attachment which we never entirely wish to conquer — such as that to a person, a garment, a book, a cell, a particular kind of food, tittle-tattle, fancies for tasting, knowing or hearing certain things, and suchlike.... While (the soul) has this there is no possibility that it will make progress in perfection, even though the imperfection be extremely small. For it is the same thing if a bird be held by a slender cord or by a stout one; since, even if it be slender, the bird will not fly away if it be not broken' (*As.* I, 11, 4).

To reiterate, the place of the emotions in the life of the Christian is to be under the control of the will. 'The strength of the soul consists in its faculties, passions and desires, all of which are governed by the will' (*As.* III, 16, 2). Yet, the will is easily undermined to do the wishes of the affections. They pressurize the will to pander to their desires and to reduce its sights to the level of meeting their needs. By so doing, they gain the mastery and become unruly, a law to themselves, and turn the soul off the path to union with God into dead ends where the desires first run and then ruin our lives. 'When these faculties, passions and desires are directed by the will towards God, and turned away from all that is not God, then the strength of the soul is kept for God, and thus the soul is able to love God with all its strength.... (But when) these four passions have the greater dominion in the soul and assail it the more vehemently, (then) the will is less strongly attached to God and more dependent on the creatures. For then it rejoices very readily at things that merit not rejoicing, hopes in that which brings no profit, grieves over that in which perchance it ought to rejoice, and fears where there is no reason for fearing. From these affections, when they are unbridled, arise in the soul all the vices and imperfections which it possesses.... And it must be known that, if one of them should become ordered and controlled by reason, the rest will become so likewise; for these four passions of the soul are so closely and intimately united to one another that the actual direction of one is the virtual direction of the others; and if one be actually recollected the other three will virtually and proportionately be recollected likewise. For, if the will rejoice in anything, it will as a result hope for the same thing to the extent of its rejoicing, and herein are virtually included grief and fear with regard to the same thing; and, in proportion as desire for these is taken away, fear and grief concerning them is likewise gradually lost and hope for them is removed.... Where thy hope is, thither will go thy joy and fear and grief; and, if thy hope returns, the others will return, and so of the rest. Wherefore thou must take note that, wheresoever one of these passions is, thither will go likewise the whole soul and the will and the other faculties, and they will live as captives to this passion, and the other three passions will be living in it also, to afflict the soul with their captivity, and not to allow it to fly upward to the liberty and rest of sweet contemplation and union.... Thou must cast from thee joys, hope, fear and grief. For, as long as these passions reign, they allow not the soul to remain in tranquillity and peace which are necessary for the wisdom which, by natural or supernatural means, it is capable of receiving' (*As.* III, 16, 2-6).

This extended section on the passions and affections has been necessary for two reasons: first, in order to rebut the widespread misunderstanding that St John is a 'cold fish', that he has no grasp of the emotional and physical drives which most human beings have, and secondly, in order to bring the whole question of the place of emotions in our progress towards union with God into relation to the place of emotions in the world at large. We can see that St John accepts and values our human nature by including within his analysis a proper place for our emotional life. He does not ask of us that we suppress or deny what is good and natural, only that it be brought into line with the will as it seeks the will of God. Indeed, we are desiring creatures, and it is fundamental to St John that desire for God, for his glory, his love, lies at the root of all progress to union with him. Without that desire of the will there can be no movement forward at all.

At the same time, his assessment of the place of emotions in our lives is an indictment of the values of our society where pressure is put upon us to indulge our emotions and to become the victims of our feelings. Modern advertising and the current philosophical climate conspire to encourage us to 'do our own thing', even if this means, as it usually does, surrendering ourselves to the gratification of immediate, self-regarding desires. Our age is antipathetic to the aims of the person who is seeking union with God, because the emphasis in society lies firmly with the self and its wants and needs. Therefore, we must be on our guard against this emphasis and resist the pressures put upon us to reduce our vision to that of the passions and affections. As we have seen, our bodily appetites, because they derive from our physical nature and are involuntary, are morally neutral and do not of themselves damage the soul in its search for union with God, provided they are under the control of the will. The function of the will, assisted by the understanding and the memory, is to govern the passions, to hold in check the natural appetites, in order to co-ordinate and direct our whole attitude and activity. Sadly, this is rarely so, and at this point we must consider the issue of sin.

St John, along with the unanimous teaching of moral

theologians, holds that sin lies wholly in the will. The disturbances in the rational soul, which are the cause of sin, arise involuntarily in the animal soul through the senses, both exterior and interior, but it is the fault of the will if it fails to control and direct the passions and desires as they arise. The natural function of our body, if left to itself, will conform to the pattern given to it by its Creator and is therefore morally good — we feel hungry because we need to eat, we have a sexual drive because we need to reproduce and to provide a strong family bonding which will sustain children during their dependent years, etc. Such actions and inclinations, as we have said, cannot harm the soul if they are properly controlled. But it is the will, and the freedom which it more or less maintains, which is faced with the moral choices we are called to make. The will is required by God to make decisions and they may be either in conformity to his will or in opposition to his will. Here, and here alone, rests the opportunity and the possibility of moral evil, which we call sin. The fault is with the will if the involuntary pressures in the sensitive part of the soul are turned to sinful ends.

Blame for sin falls fairly and squarely, and with good reason, upon the soul which commits it. Because the will is the mark, par excellence, of our humanity, it follows that sin is a human act, and therefore we, as human beings, are to reckon ourselves responsible for our sins except when sin is the result, either entirely or to a large extent, of invincible ignorance, that is, ignorance which the soul has no possible way of making good. If we say that we have been overcome by our passions, then that is often a reasonable explanation for sin, but never an excuse for sin. It is our own fault if we allow the proper ordering of our spirit to be overthrown. Of course, if we allow our will to abdicate its responsibilities regularly so that a habit of sin develops, then it may be that the sin, which is now a vice as well, becomes practically unavoidable, but the blame and the responsibility still rests with the soul for allowing the situation to develop to this critical state in the first place.

There is the additional undermining of the will, caused by what is commonly called 'original sin', which arises from our being born into a fallen world. We are enmeshed in sin from birth and this may vitiate our freedom of action, but it in no way excuses us from our responsibility before God to resist its temptations. The will is still called to maintain the harmonious working of the soul in obedience to the will of God.

It is worthwhile mentioning just one more technical term used by St John, the term 'feelings'. Surprisingly, these have no connection with the emotions. The word comes from its root verb '*sentire*', meaning to touch in the tactile sense, and is used by analogy in faculty psychology to denote an objective reference to contact from outside. It has no connotations of subjective reaction to the contact. Used in this sense we may say that we can feel the warmth of the fire, but not that we feel warm. This point is particularly important when considering what St John calls 'spiritual feelings'. These are not emotional states experienced within, but an objective act of the grace of God 'touching' the soul. What he is concerned with here is not our reactions to God's grace, but the fact that God's grace is operating upon us. We may feel nothing, or even suffer, while God touches us with his grace. That is not the point at issue. Rather, we are to accept in faith that it is the grace of God which touches us from outside ourselves. Thus St John writes, 'In order that what has been said may be the better understood, it must be noted that even as two things are perceived in the air — namely the touch thereof and the sound or whisper — so in this communication of the Spouse two other things are perceived — namely, feeling of delight, and knowledge. And even as the touch of the air is felt with the sense of touch and the whisper of the same air is heard by the ear, even so likewise the touch of the virtues of the Beloved is felt and enjoyed with the sense of touch of this soul (contact with this soul) which is in its substance; and the knowledge of these virtues of God is felt in the ear of the soul, which is the understanding' (*Cant.* B, XIV and XV, 13).

Having considered the psychology of St John in detail, we are now in a position to compare it with modern psychology. Freud and his successors have not developed their psychology from Thomist presuppositions, and this has led to many criticisms of faculty psychology. Certainly many of these objections arise from a lack of familiarity or understanding of faculty psychology, so that modern psychologists often find it difficult to grasp what is intended. In particular, one persistent objection is that the divisions within the soul presented in faculty psychology are too rigid to describe adequately the complexities of human personality, operating within the single centre of consciousness, which in modern terms we call the mind. But this objection does not take into account the truth that any description of the working of the soul is necessarily more rigid than the reality being described. The scientific method operates by dividing up and putting back together again. A frog killed and dissected on a laboratory bench is not the same as the living animal as it operates in the wild, though the dissected animal may help us to understand more clearly how and why the living frog behaves as it does in its natural habitat. St John's system is not a matter of rigid compartmentation for its own sake, but a careful diagnosis designed to reveal the complicated interplay which exists within the one mind. He sees this reality of interplay within the one mind as giving the faculties significant existence, like the colours within the one rainbow. It may not be the best possible scheme — after all, despite the truth that we are open to scientific investigation, yet we still remain a mystery to all except God, in whose image we are made — but it is true to the observable facts and is not necessarily inferior to more modern schemes developed for different purposes. St John is not dealing with the mind simply in relationship with its terrestrial environment, still less with regard to the pathological condition. Rather his scheme is intended to describe the soul's relationship with God, as the most important environment of all for human life.

The Thomist principle that 'whatever is received, is received according to the manner of the recipient' means that God deals with us according to our psychological make-up; and it is this psychological make-up, expounded by St John in his faculty psychology and brought into relationship with his theology, which gives St John the basis for his systematic writings on the way to union with God.

Another reason for the unfamiliarity of faculty psychology lies in the prevailing attitude of today which, unlike previous ages, has rejected the primacy of God. In previous ages, his sovereignty was accepted, even if the consequences of that acceptance were not adhered to. In contrast, contemporary attitudes, influenced by Freudian psychology, place the primacy of concern with the self, and tend to deny any reference beyond the self when looking for meaning to life or happiness. Personal needs, personal desires, personal wishes, personal fulfilment are the guidelines for the search for human happiness in the popular mind. This contrasts strongly with the biblical perspective and the continuous witness of the Christian tradition that God is the '*summum bonum*' and that 'the end of man is the vision of God'. We tend to look for emotional satisfaction first and foremost, thus placing ourselves in the grip of our 'passions and affections', whereas St John's analysis would ask us to look beyond emotional satisfaction to the satisfaction of 'waking up after thy likeness' as the goal of the search for human happiness. One of the ways in which modern psychology ensnares us in self is the way in which it reinforces the attention to self by using the sub-conscious unfairly as a catch-all receptacle for disposing of the inexplicable. It is assumed that if a psychological phenomenon cannot be explained then by definition it is from the sub-conscious and treated as such, whereas those who believe in the grace of God may well wish to present some other interpretation of what is happening, thus lifting the person's horizon beyond the self into the world outside, including the presence of God.

However, it has to be said at the same time that this search for self-fulfilment has occurred alongside a parallel concern for others, and the great movement in Christian circles of increased involvement with the relief of those in need has been one of the most widely accepted proofs of the validity of the Gospel. Nevertheless, the justification of this concern for the needy has two particular points which need further consideration.

The first is that post-Freudian psychology has destroyed altruism — we care for the needy because it is prudent to do so since it protects our own status in the world from attack, and because it gives us a sense of well-being to do something which benefits others. Concern for others is in danger of being part of concern with self.

Secondly, although it is true that the second great commandment is like the first, it is not identical with the first, even though much modern thought appear to think it is so. The New Testament insists that no man can love God unless he also loves his neighbour, but this is not the same thing as saying that loving one's neighbour is proof that one loves God. Nowhere in the Bible is it suggested that we should love our neighbour instead of God or as a substitute for God, but on the contrary, it is emphasized that loving God is an activity which we should do for its own sake. Indeed, we may go further and say that because of the priority of the first great commandment to love God, any act of love towards God implicitly carries with it an act of love towards neighbour and may be of more benefit to the human race than any amount of good works done for them without love for God. Without this perspective, so foreign to the modern world, yet so familiar to St John, his psychology seems pointless, and such a view is correct if we remain within the confines of the self to which Freud and his successors have consigned us.

And lastly, arising from this Godward perspective of St John's psychology, there is the point that his concern with psychopathology is directed towards the harm done to the search for human happiness by the obsession of the soul with inadequate 'goods' arising from the passions and affections and sense experience, distorting and disabling the will in its movement towards God. In contrast, modern psychopathology has no such concern and attends solely to the analysis of neurotic and psychotic components in human personality which hinder the search for human happiness, focused in the self. Therefore we would expect different analyses of the soul, designed to meet these very different ends, to come into conflict, and a massive task remains, outside the scope of this book, of assessing just how far Christians can go in incorporating Freudian and post-Freudian insights into the Christian tradition without undermining its integrity.

5. The Path to Union: First Steps

We now reach the heart of St John's thought, the purpose for which he wrote, namely, the direction of souls in the spiritual life from its beginning to its goal of union with God. And the first point to notice is that his teaching contrasts pleasantly with the complicated schemes devised by so many spiritual guides, by having a deep underlying simplicity. This simplicity is not easy simplification or shallow simplistic solutions, but is the fruit of a profound pondering upon the interaction of theology and psychology. It bears the marks both of St John's personal holiness and his awareness, born out of long experience as a director of souls, of the ways in which the grace of God fulfils our humanity and brings it to perfection.

He presents the path to union as being walked in three phases, each marked by a critical turning point in our spiritual life. These he calls conversion, the passive night of the senses and the passive night of the spirit. We may see these three points each as a gate to be passed through, though St John tends to see them as radical breaks with past experience and practice which lead to a new stage of development. Sometimes these breaks are so startling and even painful that Dom John Chapman in his spiritual letters calls them 'ligatures', likening them to the fracture of a limb. In scriptural terms, St John is describing the gospel experience which Jesus requires of us, of dying in order to live. The spiritual life is marked by the death and resurrection of Jesus being worked out in us through these three critical moments. 'For a soul to attain to the state of perfection, it has ordinarily first to pass through two principal kinds of night... the first night or purgation is the sensual part of the soul,...and the second is of the spiritual part' (*As.* I, 1, 1-2). However, St John does not dwell solely on these three points to the exclusion of all else, because each 'ligature' is intended to lead on to a new stage of development which flows from it. He emphasizes that we go through this process of dying to the past in order to find new life appropriate to our progress towards our goal. He calls these times of new life the active night of the senses and the active night of the spirit, the latter leading to spiritual betrothal and spiritual marriage, his term for full union with God. He understands these three critical 'ligatures' as steps forward on the way to union with God, retraced only by grave infidelity to God's grace or by thoroughly bad spiritual direction, or both. Therefore, although it is lacking in prudence to seek union with God without seeking spiritual direction, it is also a matter of vital importance to find a director who understands what is at stake and is a skilled 'doctor of the soul'. St Teresa complained not of a lack of holy directors, or even directors in general, but of a lack of wise directors who would be able to advise with knowledge and understanding. We need to be as discerning today as she was in sixteenth century Spain. Let us look at the way in which St John considers these three critical moments.

We begin with conversion. To be a Christian requires the birth of a living faith in our souls. For some there is a definite moment of conversion — being 'born again' — a time, a place, where the grace of God touched us and we responded to his touch with an act of dedication to him. For others, no such discernable moment is evident, but the grace of God permeates our lives until one day we realize that we are firmly committed to him and that he is the centre of our life. Yet others may find themselves converted over and over again — life can be a series of recalled moments when God's grace changed our lives, followed by periods when we draw back from him and then find ourselves drawn forward again. The range of religious experience which we gather together under the general title of conversion is as individual and as varied as there are people. What it has in common is God's initiative graciously touching our lives and our willingness to respond to his grace with a living faith, which dedicates itself to a life of obedience to the will of God and a desire for holiness and union with him. This life for beginners has many names; some call it the devout life, others call it earnestness, or yet again commitment or self-surrender.

St John calls the life that follows from conversion the active night of the senses.

But there is here a risk. To take the decision of faith seriously is to place one's life in God's hands. As such, it results in a moment when there is a void because out of a desire to serve God old securities are rejected, other loves are seen as wanting, and worldliness is revealed as not able to satisfy the deepest desires of the soul for happiness. A break is being made with the past — God's grace is pulling down our old props — and the quest for holiness begins. Here the beginner is aware, albeit imperfectly and in an immature way, that the things which are seen are transient and cannot bring lasting satisfaction. The eyes must be set firmly on the path which leads to the things which are unseen, and are believed to be eternal. It is for these unseen realities that the man of faith now risks all.

St John actually says very little about conversion as such, presumably because he was writing for those already committed to faith within the discalced reform. Nevertheless he does provide detailed analysis of the period after conversion because it is a critical stage, laying down the foundations for all further development.

Of course, theoretically this development of beginners starts at the font. Baptismal regeneration is the start of the road to union with God. But in practice, St John recognizes that the spiritual life begins in earnest only when a Christian turns to God seriously, determined to give himself to the service of God in a thorough and committed manner, being prepared to face the cost of discipleship as integral to the decision of faith. The significant point for us to recognize is that conversion does not in fact change the relationship which exists between God and us, secured in Baptism, and we should not compare the one with the other. Conversion is in effect, for those baptised, the taking seriously of the fact of regeneration.

What are the fruits of conversion? They can be summed up as enthusiasm, zeal for God. The beginner, carried forward by the grace of God, enters a time of devotion in which his life begins to be reordered around his new relationship with God. This enthusiasm is usually marked by the following signs.

First, there is the regular receiving of Holy Communion. The

Eucharist becomes full of meaning, moving the intellect and the emotions to delight in the worship of God, the offering of our lives to him, the feeding of our souls upon the Body and Blood of our Lord Jesus Christ. The beginner is finding the sweetness and joy of discipleship, the spiritual pleasures of commitment to our Lord.

Then, there is the start of vocal and mental prayer. What before had been perfunctory, or worse, becomes full of meaning, full of devotion. Acts of prayer — thanksgiving, adoration, penitence, intercession — come easily and naturally, with a sense of bringing all aspects of life into relationship with God, felt to be very near. Such prayer fills the convert with a growing awareness of dependency upon the grace of God, and with that growing awareness, the dawning of a new balance and purpose to life.

Thirdly, the beginner seeks to develop his faith through meditation. Such meditation is not of the kind based on Hinduism and its derivatives, but is designed to develop the mind of the believer, so that God's ways are more clearly understood and then systematically applied to all aspects of life. Christian meditation is the use of our intellect and imagination to increase our grasp of the truths of the Christian religion, and, as such, is the means we have of growing intellectually in our faith. The delights which flow from meditation often bring the beginner to levels of understanding about God and himself which produce rapid development in the reconstruction of life around the central point of obedience to God's will.

Fourthly, there are the other sacraments, especially for many the start of the use of the sacrament of Penance. Here again, the discovery of the joy of repentance, the assurance of forgiveness, and the power to pursue amendment of life stirs up in the beginner not only a sense of deep personal gratitude to God but also a further discovery of that dependence upon God which is our support and stay.

Fifthly, out of the life of prayer, meditation and sacramental grace, there flows a conscious attempt to live for God, to co-operate with his grace in order to restructure our life-style in obedience to his will. This is undertaken in joy, despising the pain and looking forward to victory over the old Adam whose presence in us had so vitiated our lives previous to conversion. What is being developed is an alternative life-style, the life-style of our Lord Jesus Christ.

One such traditional model for that life-style is that of the avoidance of the seven cardinal or deadly sins and the pursuit of the seven cardinal virtues. Thus, the fount of all sin, the sin of Adam and Eve, pride, is attacked with the recognition that we are not divine, but depend on God for all graces, even life itself, and therefore we need him and we need others. Vanity, arrogance, superiority, curiosity, claiming to be indispensable, are all rejected in favour of humility, shown in being honest and realistic about ourselves — that we may be acceptable to God, but we are not yet as he wants us to be. Humility as the opposite of pride requires that our self-esteem does not blind us to our own faults or to the virtues of others.

Envy, the product of the insecurity brought on by pride, is rejected because it bears grudges against others, produces intolerance, bigotry, prejudice, using the lie and the smear to destroy the good work and good name of others, creating jealousy with its demands on rights, advantages, status. In contrast, love is inculcated in the soul as the means of reducing envy and of growing in self-sacrifice, self-giving dedication to the good, the benefit, the welfare of others.

Anger, the sister of envy, is resisted as an unworthy adjunct of pride, feeding as it does upon the resentment of envy until the violence inherent in envy breaks out in physical and emotional cruelty, psychological pain, rage, assaults and even murder, the viciousness of the tongue, insulting, abusing, cursing and swearing to inflict damage, and many other terrible combinations of hatred, including hatred at a social level producing war, civil strife, class conflict, dissension and party spirit. The beginner rejects such anger in favour of meekness, that gentlest of virtues, which does not mean being a milk-sop, but being obedient to the will of God for peace. Meekness requires the courage to promote harmony out of strife, reconciliation out of enmity, communion out of dissension, agreement out of conflict. It means standing firm for God, for peace, and as such we need strength to be meek, to absorb the anger of others and not return blow for blow.

Covetousness, commonly called idolatry by St Paul, is also rejected. It is a debased desire for things as the source of happiness. This consuming vice is the misuse of God's good creation to provide us with material possessions to support our self-esteem and to provoke our neighbours to envy. It soon burns up our love for God and turns it into a love for things, thus making an idol out of what God has given us of his creation. The cure for covetousness is generosity, 'to give and not to count the cost'. Love of neighbour as well as love for God should show itself in the stewardship of our resources, turning our material benefits into a means of blessing for others and an expression of our dedication to God.

Sloth, the bosom companion of covetousness, is seen as the failure of the will to work purposefully and constructively for God. It is a mean sin which could not care less about others when there is no obvious and immediate personal gratification. The only antidote is perseverance, the willingness and effort to remain aware of others and open-hearted towards them, even and especially when there is nothing to be gained for the self. Perseverance is the way the selfish laziness of the will is overcome through persistent acts of charity towards others and acts of devotion towards God.

Sixthly, gluttony is the sin that flows from a disorderly animal appetite, the obsession with food and drink to the point of living to eat, rather than eating to live. This failure in proportion is countered by temperance, a sensible and unexciting virtue which is essential to a balanced and worthwhile life because it frees us from excess in order to give us room to work energetically for God.

Lastly, the sin of lust is, like gluttony, the result of a disorderly animal appetite, through which the person becomes over-concerned with sexual satisfaction, so that our sexual desire demands a higher place in our life than our desire for God. As such, it is a form of selfishness which operates on the level of physical gratification to the detriment of all else, including the feelings and needs of others. The opposite virtue is chastity, that practical expression of the holiness of our bodies by the right use of our sexual desires, kept within the ordering of our vocations, be it to marriage or the single state. This virtue is to be sought as the means of bringing into its proper place in God's scheme of things this particular aspect of our humanity so that it contributes constructively to the whole reordering of our lives around our service of God and our fellow human beings.

This summary of sin is inadequate to describe the full extent of human sinfulness. No list can convey the complexity and diversity of our failure before God. We begin with pride and in one sense we never leave that sin — all other sins emerge from this one. The pride of Adam and Eve, in desiring to become like God, knowing good and evil, led them to disobedience, and only a full-hearted obedience to the will of Christ will finally extinguish the sin of pride within us. Obedience to the will of Christ, expressed in and through the life of the Church, is the cornerstone of the alternative life-style we are called to lead. We are called to live within the common life of the community of faith in good conscience, in contrast to Adam and Eve, thrust out of the garden of Eden in anguish and bitterness of soul. And this obedience has to be worked out in terms of our actions, our thoughts and our speech; it must include what we have failed to do for good as well as the harm we have done; there are corporate and institutional aspects of sin and virtue as well as personal individual concerns — the struggle for economic, political and social justice, for world peace, for international reconciliation and compassion, are examples of where the Christian life-style leads us in the reformation of manners required by our turning from sin to virtue.

In terms of the intellectual faculties of the soul, the understanding is being fed through the senses with information about God that is forming the intellectual foundation of faith; the memory is being supplied through sensual experience of God's grace with material upon which to begin to build hope; the will is finding the sensual delights of devotion and service the basis upon which to foster a rudimentary love for God.

However, the scope for self-deception at this stage is enormous. Carried along by enthusiasm, the soul is liable to many mistakes, often zealously pursued mistakenly as the will of God. There is a great need for guidance lest the soul be misled by its own immaturity, leading to unrealistic self-assessment and consequent disappointment at setbacks. The loss of souls at this stage is only too frequent, due to a mistaken confidence that they are nearer to union than they really are and an unacknow-ledged dependence not on God but on the senses.

Therefore although St John does not give detailed direction concerning the sacraments, prayer, meditation and good works, he does spend considerable time discussing the pitfalls that lie in the path of beginners at this stage in their journey. The basic point which he wishes to make is this: the reformation of life after conversion consists in redirecting the desires and pleasures of the senses away from the vices of sin towards virtue and devotion to God. This means that the delights of the senses con-tinue to operate, but in the direction of God and not in the direction of self. Pleasure is found in serving God rather than oneself; enthusiasm is stirred up to worship God rather than for self-centred pursuits. This is an active phase in the spiritual life in which we co-operate with the grace of God to wean our sensual nature from indulgence in self on to the more solid food of faith. But the senses continue to play a central part in our dedication to God, and herein lies the danger. We may redirect them but we still need them as the means of expressing our devotion. What we have is a reflex reaction — devotion to God means instant spiritual satisfaction.

Also, another characteristic of the beginner is the need for 'visual aids' to help devotion because of the strong attachment to and dependence on material things still retained by the soul. Thus, the beginner is attracted to crucifixes, holy pictures, ritual acts, the beauty of worship, and so on. Attachment to a particular statue, particular gifts of the Spirit, or even fervent hymn-singing, are all signs of immaturity which easily dresses itself up as advanced devotion. Clearly, we are not concerned here with idolatry, because the soul is dedicated to what is represented, not the aid itself, no more than rereading a letter from a friend makes the letter a substitute for the friend — there is little risk of loving the letter and forgetting the friend! Similarly, it would be ridiculous and foolish if Christians be-came attached to crucifixes, for example, to the exclusion of their Lord, whom they represent. The 'visual aid' is there to help the soul to express its delight in God and when this happens the aid is totally beneficial in its effects. However, the dangers of such aids to the soul reveal themselves only too clearly when the beginner is disturbed and finds devotion flagging when deprived of these things. Is this not the root of so much resistance to new liturgical forms?

This early time is one when many 'spiritual vices' emerge, which St John deals with at length, because they easily invert themselves to appear to be positive virtues. For example, the beginner may see his enthusiasm as bringing great spiritual gains; this stirs up admiration for his enthusiasm; the resulting loss of humility severely damages his ability to correct his inadequate assessment of his progress towards God. Therefore, in order to make genuine progress, the beginner must recognize that he has made but one step along the right path, namely, the realignment of the senses away from gross sin in the direction of devotion to God. He has yet to make the second step of maintaining that devotion without the support of those sensual delights. The move to come is from loving God for the pleasures it brings to continuing to love God when those pleasures are taken away.

True, this first phase is a 'night' because the beginner moves by faith and not by sight, because God is incomprehensible, and because there is some deprivation to the sensual soul through learning detachment from selfish pursuits in order to seek attachment to God, but this active night of the senses does not have that intensity of deprivation which loss of the sensual delights of devotion will bring. The soul is not yet really tested in its love for God because so far the stripping away has only been of sensual hindrances to devotion, and those are gladly surrendered in the enthusiasm of conversion. Further stripping away needs far more courage.

Conversion does not produce immediate holiness. One decision is not enough to win God. The active night of the senses which follows conversion is a period of reform in which the priorities of the sensual soul are assessed, found wanting, and changed. Our passions are checked lest they lead us into sin and channelled towards virtue. But over and above that, because the information received by the rational soul through the animal soul cannot be the means to union with God, the demand is implicit that even delight in virtue and grief at sin are not

70

sufficient to bring lasting happiness. What is needed is something more fundamental, detachment from the effects of the passions and affections, so that we cease to depend upon them even for spiritual delights and devotion. We need to become indifferent to the pleasures and pains of experience, so that although we may enjoy them or be hurt by them, we shall not be swayed by them or tempted to place them above our love for God. What is good may be enjoyed as good, but is no substitute for the author of goodness himself; what is evil may be suffered as evil, but is no cause for despair in the good providence of the Almighty. We are to detach ourselves from the cravings of the animal soul for sensual satisfaction, even of a devotional kind, by attaching ourselves to God and his goodness towards us as the source of our deepest fulfilment, yet to come in the consummation of our journey in union with him.

This stage in our spiritual journey may last weeks, months, years or even a whole lifetime, depending on how seriously we take the consequences of our conversion and just how deeply the major sins are rooted in the soul. God's grace is present for us to make progress, but it requires our active co-operation and willingness to enter into the experience of 'night', albeit of a preliminary intensity, before any movement forward occurs. Nevertheless, St John envisages that every Christian who is serious about his faith should achieve sufficient development in his soul through the active night of the senses to reach the second stage marked by a new 'ligature' which he calls the passive night of the senses.

6. The Path to Union: Making Progress

The second critical turning point in our journey to union with God is called passive because what happens to the soul is entirely the work of the grace of God and the soul has no part to play in what it experiences. God acts to bring to an end the active night of the senses by plunging the soul into the unknown where it cannot use its faculties to make any response to its new God-given situation. Thus St John writes: 'In order that we may understand this the better, we must know that the state of beginners comprises meditation and discursive acts. In this state, it is necessary for the soul to be given material for meditation, and to make interior acts on its own account, and take advantage of the spiritual heat and fire which come from sense; this is necessary in order to accustom the senses and delights to good things, so that, by being fed with this delight, they may become detached from the world. But when this has been to some extent effected, God begins to bring the soul into the state of contemplation... which happens when the discursive acts and the meditation of the soul itself cease, and the first favours and sweetness of sense cease likewise, so that the soul cannot meditate as before, or find any help in the senses; for the senses remain in a state of aridity, inasmuch as their treasure is transformed into spirit, and no longer falls within the capacity of sense. And, as all the operations which the soul can perform on its own account naturally depend upon sense only, it follows that God is the agent in this state and the soul is the recipient; for the soul behaves only as one that receives and as one in whom these things are being wrought; and God as One that gives and acts and as One that works these things in the soul, giving it spiritual blessings in contemplation, which is divine knowledge and love in one — that is, a loving knowledge, wherein the soul has not to use its natural acts and meditations, for it can no longer enter into them as before. It follows that at this time the soul must be led in a way entirely contrary to the way wherein it was led at first. If formerly it was given material for meditation, and practised meditation, this material must now be taken from it and it must not meditate; for, as I say, it will be unable to do so even though it would, and it will become distracted. And if formerly it sought sweetness and fervour, and found it, now it must neither seek it nor desire it, for not only will it be unable to find it through its own diligence, but it will rather find aridity, for it turns from the quiet and peaceful blessings which were secretly given to its spirit, to the work that it desires to do with sense; and thus it will lose the one and not obtain the other, since no blessings are now given to it by means of sense as they were formerly. Wherefore in this state the soul must never have meditation imposed upon it, nor must it perform any act, nor strive after sweetness or fervour; for this would be to set an obstacle in the way of the principal agent who, as I say, is God. For God secretly and quietly infuses into the soul loving knowledge and wisdom without any intervention of specific acts, although sometimes he specifically produces them in the soul for some length of time. And the soul has then to walk with loving awareness of God, without performing specific acts, but conducting itself, as we have said, passively, and have no diligence of its own, but possessing this simple, pure and loving awareness, as one that opens his eyes to the awareness of love' (*Lvg.Fl*. III, 30-31). This long passage is worth quoting in full because it eloquently describes the heart of the change and the means of responding to it. As such, it cannot be bettered in its simplicity and clarity, though it does not describe the attendant confusion and sense of deprivation which often accompanies this 'ligature'. We need to explore in more detail both the factors which immediately precede and surround this move into the passive night of the senses and the consequences of the move as contemplation sets in, displacing meditation and vocal and mental prayer.

Since all knowledge comes through the senses and passes on to the intellectual faculties of the spirit, any loss in the functioning of the sensual soul plunges the spirit into confusion. This deprivation causes a deepening of the 'night' in which the soul lives, generally removing previous signposts and directions for following God set up by the spirit on the basis of sense information received. The grace of God is again pulling down old props — the help that comes from the senses in the practice of devotion — in order that we should die to that particular dependency and move forward in the darkness of faith to a new stage in our journey to union with God. In St Bernard's terms it is the move from loving God for our own sakes to loving God for his sake. We are being required to love God not for the good things he gives us but for himself alone.

What is happening in this 'ligature' is the reorientation of the spirit to live 'darkly', detached from the sense information fed to it from the animal soul. The considerable spiritual pleasures which have compensated the soul during the active night of the senses for the loss of the pleasures of the old Adam are now taken away by God. The passions and affections, even though trained and reorientated towards God, now cease to function; intellectual joy derived from the fruits of meditation collapses; the use of words and ideas in prayer becomes impossible and all pleasure in prayer ceases. All that has been achieved since conversion, often at considerable personal cost, seems to be in danger, or a waste of effort. Is the priority of God real after all?

This is again a moment of great risk, where the ruin of souls is often caused by bad spiritual direction. Many are forced back to exercises which they can no longer perform; many are put under an obedience which is blind and ignorant causing the stunting of their souls. Such bad direction causes many to lapse into unbelief through disappointment that nothing more is offered to them than the repetition of dead forms, while others settle down to an arid, misguided duty which holds them in an infantile dependency upon the director and prevents progress towards Christian maturity.

What needs to be recognized is that what is happening is taking place in a 'dark night'. The change that is being wrought in us by God cannot be understood in terms of intellectual certainty or conclusive rational proof, but can only be interpreted by faith. He is asking us again to risk all on the things that are unseen and to do that by detaching ourselves from the tangible in favour of the intangible. The result is usually neither comforting nor comfortable. With the onset of the passive night of the senses, the darkness intensifies and considerable distress often results. Depending on the sort of people we are, the 'ligature' may be sudden and totally bewildering or it may be gradual and fairly gentle. Diagnosing what is happening is not too difficult for a skilled spiritual director but can be seriously misread by an unskilled one, causing, as we have said, considerably more anguish than is necessary, stunted development, misplaced submission to authority, and even despair and loss of faith.

We can describe the process in principle by considering two types of person. First, there is the person who keeps his intellectual faculties very separate from his passions and affections. Such a person may find more pleasure in meditation than in prayer. The understanding is able to operate in a fairly cut and dried manner, analysing the truths of the Christian faith efficiently, and the will, seeing its Christian duty, acts resolutely to put insight into practice. Feelings may not be very evident and are generally kept under control as disruptive. This may lead to a reluctance to move from meditation into prayer because of the difficulties of quietening the intellect, which tends to freewheel, and because poor imagination leads to prayer by rote. Public worship provides intellectual stimulation but there is little accompanying emotional content. When God moves such a person on into the passive night of the senses the intellectual faculties are thrown into total disarray. The mental suffering of such a person can be most severe both because of the suddenness and completeness of the act and because the passions and affections are ill-equipped to provide any compensating consolation. The result is that meditation ceases abruptly; the mind cannot think, nothing 'adds up', all satisfaction is destroyed, all sense of direction is lost, God seems unreal, all intellectual constructs supporting faith crash to the ground. For such a person, this is a moment of supreme danger, faced in utter darkness — a 'ligature' indeed.

In contrast, the other type of person who helps us to understand what is happening in the passive night of the senses is the one where the passions and affections react very freely with the intellectual faculties. In this case the soul delights in the beauty and enthusiasm of public worship, enjoys mental and vocal prayer developing it imaginatively to provide a rich satisfying matrix of intellectual and emotional interplay, but often finds meditation tedious or not very helpful because the use of a vivid imagination is not followed through with much interest in rigorous intellectual analysis. Such a person is an instinctive, intuitive Christian who feels the things of faith in a direct and yet poorly articulated manner. When God moves such a person into the passive night of the senses, the intellectual distress may be minimal, but the emotional loss coming from the failure of imagination and the collapse of enthusiasm at public worship and prayer can hurt. However, because of the free interaction between the intellectual faculties and the passions and affections, the move into this new phase often happens slowly, in stages, so that there is a transition period when there are times of contemplation but there are also other times when mental and vocal prayer and meditation are possible. In this case, there is none of the suddenness and completeness of the act, but rather the soul moves gently and peacefully into the habit of contemplation, learning to adjust slowly to the new demand that God's grace requires of it.

We know from her writings that St Teresa was of this second type, and we may guess from his writings that St John was much more like the first. Most of us fall somewhere in between and need the direction of someone who knows us sufficiently well to recognize the psychological nuances of our souls.

As we have seen from the writings of St John, the nub of the issue at this stage is meditation and mental and vocal prayer. Therefore, four basic questions need to be asked of a person who believes himself to be entering the passive night of the senses. These are:

> Does the person under direction still wish to pray?

> Can he use mental and vocal prayer?

> Can he use his intellectual faculties, his imagination and his passions and affections to meditate?

> Is he in serious sin?

If the answers to these questions are affirmative to the first, indicating continuing commitment to faith in God, and negative to the others, indicating that there is no moral impediment to the free access of the grace of God in the soul and the direct action of that grace upon the soul to incapacitate its faculties in the pursuit of discursive reasoning, then that person is entering the passive night of the senses. If any of the answers is otherwise, then that person is still in the active night of the senses and needs direction appropriate to that state, be it further exhortation to repentance and amendment of life, or more instruction in the faith or additional material for meditation and prayer. All four conditions must be fulfilled for the soul to move safely into contemplation, leaving the support of the senses behind, and preparing to transform the working of the intellectual faculties of the spirit without the aid of the information provided by the animal soul. To attempt this move too soon is to court disaster — it is not a development which we can bring about for ourselves but is a gift of the grace of God made in our souls when he chooses to do so. We are called to prepare ourselves for it during the active night of the senses, but the start of the passive night of the senses is in God's hands not ours. It comes with the ending of natural ability and moves ahead under the sole guidance of supernatural grace.

St John makes it quite clear that the change in direction lies in the surrender of meditation and mental and vocal prayer and their replacement by contemplation. Again, this is not achieved over night. The soul needs time to adjust to the change. For many, there is the intense pain of the 'ligature', the feeling of emptiness, of being stripped, of being abandoned by God, of disorientation through the failure of the senses to operate. Getting used to the new life usually takes time. The question now is not so much 'How can I pray?' as 'How can I meet my desire to be with God?'

To answer this question, we must first acknowledge that all our 'knowing about' God, developed by meditation, is not good enough to bring us into that close 'knowing' which God wishes for us. Faith remains radically distinct from knowledge. Therefore, in the new and more intense darkness of this passive night of the senses, faith must act without its usual sensual props, by risking all on God's will for us to have us for himself in a relationship called union, which is beyond intellectual knowledge. This union is not yet, but the abandonment of intellectual knowledge as an inadequate means to union is the next step on the way to our goal. This act of faith requires that we simplify our approach to God, or rather, acknowledge that God himself has made that simplification necessary because he has removed the ability to continue in the old way. The soul is not to yearn for mental and vocal prayer; it is not to try to meditate; it is simply to rest in the darkness of this night, getting used to the darkness as its new environment. It needs to take care not to seek to force God to make his presence known as before by attempting to stir up former feelings of devotion, but must be still, attentive to the presence of God, hidden in the darkness waiting to make itself known to faith. The soul is to begin a life of simple waiting, to grow accustomed to that intuitive, obscure, face-to-face relationship with God, which is called contemplation and of which any articulation results in a wooden constraint being put upon an ineffable reality. To seek an explanation in intellectual terms to satisfy the understanding leads to loss of the very thing which we are trying to describe.

The risk is great — it entails the loss of all dependence on spiritual pleasures — but the prize makes it worthwhile. 'Where your treasure is, there will your heart be also.' This contemplation is not the easy irrationality of eastern mysticism but the orderly change of 'knowing about' God into 'knowing' God which gathers up the first stage and fulfils it in a movement of grace in which nothing is lost, so that all that has gone before is transfigured in the darkness.

It is worth repeating that this transition during the passive night of the senses takes time. Getting used to the new way of knowing comes gradually. But once the darkness becomes familiar, and the shock and pain subside, then contemplation develops more and more naturally, becomes progressively under the control of the will, so that 'praying without ceasing' becomes a habit of the soul. Once the period of settling down is over, the passive night of the senses comes to an end and the orderly work of continuing growth in detachment can begin in yet another way, within what St John calls the active night of the spirit. This will involve the reorientation of the intellectual faculties of the understanding, memory and will towards the will of God, and must now be considered in more detail.

The arrival of the active night of the spirit is the start of what, for most of us, is the work of the rest of our lifetime. The third 'ligature', yet to be described, is not granted to everyone, and for the vast majority the life of contemplation, accompanied by the continuing reorientation of the intellectual faculties, will take up the remaining years of our earthly life. What is being sought now is a union of faith, hope and love, as the next step towards that full union which for most of us God grants beyond the veil and gateway of death.

Of course, during this stage in the journey towards union, the habits and virtues of the active night of the senses are not lost. We continue to practise them with a detachment from sense which means we are not swayed either way by pleasure or pain. The sacramental life remains the foundation of our relationship with God — regular receiving of Holy Communion and use of the other sacraments, especially Penance, are still to be part of our rule of life. But we no longer look for the sensual delights previously experienced, but now taken away. We continue to practise a life of virtue, rejecting temptation to sin and ordering all things around obedience to the will of Christ and his Church. But we do so without any desire for or dependence on sensual satisfaction or distress at sensual deprivation. We are not looking for special illumination or insight. Detachment is all; the senses cease to dominate; we are largely freed from their demand for recognition and gratification. Now, with the help of God's grace, we are in a position to consolidate the intellectual faculties upon their relationship with God, released, by and large, from the pressure derived from the conflicting demands of the exterior and interior corporeal senses. The task to hand is 'stripping the spirit of all spiritual imperfections and desires for the possession of spiritual things... putting to rest this house of the spiritual part, and of being able to enter this interior darkness, which is spiritual detachment from all things whether sensual or spiritual, and leaning on pure faith alone and an ascent thereby to God' (*As.* II, 1, 1).

To achieve this we need to empty our spiritual faculties through the pursuit of the three theological virtues — faith in the understanding, hope in the memory and love in the will. These three theological virtues each cause the appropriate faculty to enter into a state of darkness in which detachment from spiritual possessions takes place. 'Faith, in the understanding, causes an emptiness and darkness with respect to the understanding; hope, in the memory, causes emptiness of all possessions; and charity causes emptiness in the will and detachment from all affection and from rejoicing in all that is not God.... Faith, although it brings certainty to the understanding, brings it not clearness, but obscurity.... As to hope, there is no doubt but that it renders the memory empty and dark with respect both to things below and things above.... Charity causes emptiness in the will with respect to all things, since it obliges us to love God above them all; which cannot be unless we withdraw our affection from them all in order to set it wholly upon God' (*As*. II, 6, 2-3). By these means the soul attains 'to the possession of that detachment and emptiness in its faculties which is required for simple union' (*As*. II, 5, 11).

What is happening in the active night of the spirit is the simplification of the soul's desiring upon God. The understanding, having been fed in the past by meditation and now finding that source of information closed to it, settles down in the habit of faith. This does not mean that the soul ceases to study theology, or that it does not need theology to inform itself about faith; rather the insights of theology are weighed against the intuitive knowing that the darkness of faith contains. Recognizing that intellectual knowledge is not the proximate or proportionate means of knowing God in union, the soul rests content in the obscure knowing which resides in the habit of faith. The understanding is content to be detached from clearly formulated knowledge about God and directs its energies towards the virtue of faith, practised in a life of contemplation and trust in God. 'The more profound and clear are the things of God in themselves, the more completely unknown and obscure they are to us.... Among all created things, and things that belong to the understanding, there is no ladder whereby the understanding can attain to this high Lord' (*As*. II, 8, 4). We are moving from using a method of prayer and meditation which is concerned with technique into a simple intuitive relationship with God.

This darkness in the understanding, caused by the loss of natural knowledge and apprehensions, is not a blank darkness but 'the obscurity of faith wherein the Divinity is concealed, when It communicates Itself to the soul; which will be ended when, as St Paul says, that which is in part shall be ended, which is this darkness of faith, and that which is perfect shall come, which is the Divine light' (*As.* II, 9, 3). However, the fact that natural knowledge no longer operates does not mean that super-natural knowledge cannot inform the understanding, meaning direct knowledge not mediated through the senses. These communications we must consider later in order to understand how to assess their value and their place in our progress towards union, lest they produce in the soul more harm than good.

What we have described of the understanding and faith, applies equally to the memory and hope. We are to cease to regard sensual delights as the stay of our memory, but empty the memory of all such possessions in order to hold fast to God in hope. The ability of the imagination in particular to feed the memory with the remembrance of the good things of God's grace in the past is ignored and the memory, deprived of this sensual support, reorientates itself to the pursuit of the virtue of hope, 'causing it to rise above itself — that is, above all clear knowledge and apprehensible possession — to the supreme hope of God, who is incomprehensible' (*As.* III, 2, 3). Again, the move is from what is external and reliant upon technique into living in the present reality of God with us, hidden as this is. When this takes place at the beginnings of union, the loss of the imaginary forms which have fed the memory causes this faculty to become inert, its self-awareness suspended during the moments of union. 'Sometimes this oblivion of the memory and suspension of the imagination reach such a point, because of the union of the memory with God, that a long time passes without the soul's perceiving it, or knowing what has taken place during that period' (*As.* III, 2, 6). However, this is a temporary phenomenon which disappears when contemplation becomes habitual. To advance in this reorientation of the memory towards hope, the soul must take care not to seek to store up or collect in its memory any impressions, however apparently worthwhile, from the senses. Again, if the memory is settled in the virtue of hope, then these sensual experiences cease to matter, but supernatural impressions, coming without the help

81

of the senses, can continue to enter the memory, and need to be tackled carefully lest they undermine the hope that unites the memory with God.

Thirdly, the emptying of the will crowns this stage in the soul's progress towards union with God. Having been fed by the understanding and the memory with information designed to promote the reformation of manners required by beginners during the active night of the senses, the will now ceases to delight in that reformation as an end in itself, or be swayed by the deprivation caused by the rejection of sin in favour of virtue. Instead it continues to maintain that reformation for the sake of God alone. Its delight is now solely in God. Therefore the will directs its energies towards loving God for his own sake and detaching itself from all other loves as inadequate in themselves to bring the soul to union with God in the will. As before, relationship with God becomes all-important and regulates our desire to love God in a way which has previously been impossible.

The vital place that the will has in the reordering of the priorities of the soul is put thus by St John: 'We should have accomplished nothing by the purgation of the understanding in order to ground it in the virtue of faith, and by the purgation of the memory in order to ground it in hope, if we purged not the will also according to the third virtue, which is charity' because 'the strength of the soul consists in its faculties, passions and desires, all of which are governed by the will. Now when these faculties, passions and desires are directed by the will towards God, and turned away from all that is not God, then the strength of the soul is kept for God, and thus the soul is able to love God with all its strength' (As. III, 16, 1-2).

The need for the will to bring to order the passions and affections during the active night of the senses is now completed by growing detachment from these reordered delights, so that not even they distract the will from seeking a union of love with God alone. All other loves must have within themselves a core of detachment because the final and total attachment which the will seeks is solely to God. Love for God is to become the fixed habit of the will and the integrating power around which the faith of the understanding and the hope of the memory coinhere to produce a union of faith, hope and love with God in these intellectual faculties, together with marked progress towards holiness and the image of Christ in the believer. But again, although we may believe that the senses are stilled, nevertheless, disturbances do continue to arise in the soul, some of natural origin, and some of supernatural origin, and the soul must be prepared to know what to do about them. To these and the other dangers besetting the understanding, the memory and the will during the active night of the spirit we must now turn.

7. The Path to Union: Diversions and Distractions

During the active night of the spirit, the intellectual faculties continue to operate through the three theological virtues, even though increasingly detached from the exterior and interior corporeal senses, operating naturally. However, the fact that this is so does not prevent supernatural influence being brought to bear upon them. St John sees these supernatural influences upon the intellectual faculties as of two kinds, from God and from Satan. The spirit is open to influence from the divine and the demonic and it is essential to recognize this state of affairs if a realistic assessment of our experience during contemplation is to be made, and appropriate steps taken to maintain the faculties on the right path. Furthermore, there is a complicating factor in the perception of supernatural influence, which is our human nature. The supernatural, be it for good or for ill, operates through our nature. Therefore as long as our nature is imperfect even divine grace can be perceived in a distorted way, so that what God gives us and what we understand him to be giving us may not be apprehended as the same. And what is true of divine grace is, *a fortiori*, even more true of demonic influence, where the combination of Satanic malevolence with human sin may lead to all sorts of spiritual self-deception, evil and loss.

It must be stressed that any attempt to seek or force special insights or illuminations is not only doomed to failure, but also highly dangerous and delusory. We are not to expect them or desire them. Indeed, many people rarely experience supernatural knowledge of any kind and live in a simple, intuitive relationship with God, which is both certain and obscure, and full of a quiet peace and joy which sustains their hope and inspires their love. Such a gracious life with God is enough to bring us to union with him. However, for the sake of completeness, and because St John himself spends considerable time and energy systematically analysing the nature and effects of supernatural influence upon the soul, we must consider this aspect of the active night of the spirit. There are here serious pitfalls for the rash and the headstrong, much heartache for the foolish and many delusions for the proud.

Because the analysis is rather technical it may be that the following material is better suited for directors who wish to have a framework for understanding St John's teaching than for the ordinary reader. Also, we must remember that no book, by itself, can guide us in our quest for union with God. We need someone else to help us and befriend us on our journey, and never more so than at this point of ambiguity and potential danger. What follows is necessarily rather compressed, and therefore the saint's original analysis should always be consulted when in doubt.

In brief we are considering the three faculties of the spirit as open to influence in the form of supernatural knowledge in the understanding and memory and supernatural blessings in the will, and seeking the means of benefiting from their grace when of God and avoiding their temptation to sin when of Satan.

St John describes supernatural knowledge entering the understanding through two routes — the corporeal and the spiritual. There are two kinds of corporeal supernatural knowledge, one received through the exterior corporeal senses and the other through the interior corporeal senses. Spiritual supernatural knowledge also falls into two kinds, one being clear knowledge given to the spirit, without the aid of the corporeal senses, such as visions, locutions, spiritual feelings and revelations; and the other being that obscure and general type of knowledge which is contemplation. The process of movement through the active night of the spirit consists in systematically detaching the understanding from each of these in turn, beginning with the first.

Corporeal supernatural knowledge comes from the heightening of the five senses of the body beyond their natural ability, resulting in the following symptoms. The sight may produce visions of saints, of angels, or of other apparitions from heaven or hell, bright lights and so on. The ears may hear messages from such visions, or words spoken without seeing the person who utters them. The senses of smell and taste may become conscious of sweet perfumes or flavours. The sense of touch may experience delightful physical feelings.

Such sensations are fairly common and ordinary at this stage of the soul's journey. But all of them, whether good or bad, must be rejected. We are not to admit them, still less come to rely on them, as spiritual aids. Rather we must flee from them, refusing even to make an assessment of whether they are good or evil. The temptation here is to let sensual things make the running, so that their estimate of what is good for the soul overrides the discretion of the spirit. But the fallacy which entraps our exterior corporeal senses is that their estimate of spiritual benefit lies at the level of what the experience feels like, not whether it is advancing us towards union with God. Indeed, St John writes, 'Bodily sense is as ignorant of spiritual things as is a beast of rational things, and even more so' (*As.* II, 11, 2). Furthermore, the danger of deception is compounded by the possibility of the influence of Satan, often disguised as an angel of light. This is the level at which he has greatest sway because of the ease with which he can deceive the soul through sense experience. 'The more attention (the soul) pays to such things, the farther it strays from the true way and means, which are faith' (*As.* II, 11, 4). In addition, entertaining such supernatural sensual delights can produce the insidious notion in our understanding that these experiences imply that we are of particular importance in the eyes of God — an act of pride, straight from Satan, destroying all progress in humility. Satan is perfectly capable of producing all the sweet delights the exterior corporeal senses could desire, and ruin the soul in the process. Therefore all representations and feelings must, as a matter of principle, always and at once be rejected as of no importance for our relationship with God. Having or not having them is no test of our standing in his sight. If some are from God, he will not be offended, because such a rejection does not prevent him from doing what he desires in the soul. Any supernatural knowledge of this kind which comes from God carries with it grace from God which enters the soul to its benefit and will bear fruit even if the knowledge itself is rejected. Thus if a vision of a saint brings to the soul a sense of renewed faith, then rejection of the vision still leaves the renewed faith in place in the soul. So, we are not to deliberate whether to accept or reject such knowledge but always to remain detached from it. It comes to us without the consent of the will and without our own effort, and if from God brings a blessing to us. We receive both the knowledge and the blessing passively, but choose not to retain the knowledge itself. In the same way what comes from Satan does so without the consent of the will to bring its own gift, this time trouble, aridity, vanity, presumption and other deadly disturbances in the spirit. Yet the influence of Satan is not as effective as the grace of God because it needs the consent of the will to move from being a temptation into bringing about sin. Therefore, these disturbances do not persist unless the soul lacks courage and prudence. We are to stand firm against them, no matter how attractive or delightful they appear to be. If they are of God, they will always do good to the soul; if of Satan, they will only harm it once the will consents to entertain the temptation. Therein lies the advantage of grace over demonic influence.

To make the point even clearer we need to consider the six ways in which the soul is put at a disadvantage if it entertains and accepts corporeal supernatural knowledge. First, faith diminishes as dependency upon this form of knowledge increases. We come to rely on 'special' religious experiences as the form of our religion.

Secondly, such knowledge holds back the spirit from desiring union with God because the soul seeks to rest in the delights of the senses instead of encouraging the spirit to seek what is beyond sense.

Thirdly, the soul becomes attached to these things and makes no further steps towards letting them go and becoming detached in the spirit.

Fourthly, the sensual aspect of such knowledge becomes increasingly important — the soul begins to crave for supernatural sensual experience — and as a consequence the inward grace received becomes increasingly secondary. This leads to greatly reduced benefit in the spirit because it is the senses that are being pampered.

Fifthly, the soul becomes possessive of such knowledge,

claiming it as belonging to itself, and so begins to lose the favours of God. To accept them is in itself not to profit from them, because it means we are seeking favours, which is precisely what we should not be doing. And in any case, it is presumptuous of the soul to take upon itself the opinion that the knowledge received is of God anyway — far better to reject all than to be deceived.

Sixthly, readiness to accept supernatural knowledge of this kind opens the door to Satan. He knows perfectly well how to disguise his influence, pretending to be good. Therefore we cannot risk the progress we have made by entertaining for a moment the material presented to the understanding in such a supernatural way. All must be rejected as inadequate to bring the understanding into union with God — only faith can do this, even supernatural knowledge is unable to do so.

It is important to recognize that information from the exterior corporeal senses, received supernaturally, has led to the downfall of many who cling to gross visions, messages and sensual delights, and are beguiled by them as substitutes for union with God. They may be of God or of Satan, they may be experienced with or without distortion by our own personalities; either way, all clear knowledge must be rejected as inadequate, unable to settle the understanding in the practice of faith. To reject all is to follow the safe course — in process the demonic influences are rejected together with their unsettling and harmful effects on the soul, but the grace of God still bears fruit in the soul, even though the knowledge accompanying that grace is rejected as unhelpful to the leading of the understanding along the path to union with God by faith. We must be resigned to living with the understanding darkened and not seek to relieve that darkness with distracting and deceptive knowledge, however appealing it may appear to be.

This analysis of the dangers of corporeal supernatural knowledge has been set out at length because it exemplifies the approach to all other forms of knowledge received supernaturally by the understanding. These can be summarized as follows.

The next form of supernatural knowledge is that of the interior corporeal senses, the imagination and the fancy. Here grace or demonic influence work upon these interior senses to produce the supernatural equivalent of meditation, that is, the revealing to the understanding of imaginary visions, not through thinking about aspects of our faith but passively by the direct intervention of the supernatural. This supernatural imaginary knowledge is beyond the natural powers of the interior senses, even though it uses the same sorts of exterior sense material as the imagination does when acting naturally. The sort of knowledge referred to here includes such things as Isaiah's vision of God in glory in the temple, the many visions in the book of Daniel, the dreams of Pilate's wife, and the transfiguration of Christ. The effects are in principle the same as those produced by meditation, but because the visions are supernatural in origin, their effects are in fact more powerful and more influential. Also because they are more interior than the external supernatural visions, they make a far deeper impression than those. But all forms of supernatural knowledge from the imagination and the fancy are to be rejected by the understanding for exactly the same reasons as set out for the rejection of corporeal supernatural knowledge. We cannot risk admitting demonic influence and its destructive consequences into the understanding through the gateway of the imagination and the fancy. Even what comes from God may lead us to deceive ourselves. We reject all such knowledge because it is not a proximate and proportionate means to union. God's grace is not hindered in its operation on the soul by rejection of such knowledge, but rejection does eliminate the influence of Satan before it disturbs the soul.

If this is so, then we have to ask why God permits us to be given this supernatural knowledge in the exterior and interior senses of the animal soul. It is because of the principle that God's grace operates upon us in accordance with our nature. The movement of grace from conversion to union is a systematic transformation of every aspect of our make-up, gathering up the powers of the soul as we progress, until the complete transfiguration of the whole human being is achieved. Therefore the supernatural, as well as the natural, working of each part of the soul has to be transformed, as necessary, by grace, and this is what is happening at this step on the way to union. The exterior and interior senses are being transformed and put to silence, naturally and supernaturally, in accordance with our individual needs and characteristics as persons, so that the understanding comes to rely on faith alone. This is the appropriate moment for such sense experience to be rejected, and it is a phase to be gone through and maintained in order to accustom ourselves to this level of detachment. What has to be preserved is not the visions, voices, perfumes, tastes and feelings generated in the senses supernaturally, but the increase in virtue and good works which they produce.

Now we can move on to the supernatural knowledge which enters the understanding directly without the use of the senses, looking first at the forms of clear knowledge under the four headings of visions, locutions, spiritual feelings and revelations. Here we are describing forms of awareness or inspiration in the understanding, which can only be described by analogy. Visions are communications which correspond to sight in the senses although nothing is actually seen in the understanding; locutions, to hearing, although nothing is actually heard; spiritual feelings, to smelling, tasting, touching, although nothing is actually experienced of those senses; revelations are communications which correspond to the results of meditation produced by the imagination working with the understanding, although both the imagination and understanding are dark and no meditation actually occurs. Indeed, all the senses and the understanding are dark and passive when intellectual supernatural knowledge enters the spirit; it requires no work from the soul, but comes to it without any voluntary act to seek it or prepare for it, entirely from outside, that is from God or Satan. Such knowledge is the irruption of the unknown directly into the understanding, without its co-operation or desire.

Examples of such intellectual supernatural knowledge are as follows. Visions may be either of corporeal things, relating to either heaven or earth, e.g. St Benedict's vision of the whole world and St John's vision of the heavenly Jerusalem, or of incorporeal things, such as Moses's and Elijah's visions of God, or of angels and souls departed this life — this type of vision often goes with 'out of the body' experiences such as St Paul describes in 2 Corinthians. Both kinds, but especially the second, are fleeting and rare.

Locutions fall into three categories which St John calls successive, formal and substantial. Successive locutions are teachings about aspects of the Christian faith, e.g. concerning the last judgement or the presence of Christ in the sacrament of the Eucharist. People experiencing these often say: 'God spoke to me...', 'God answered me...', whether this is the case or not. Successive locutions are always built upon the material of meditation considered by a recollected spirit, even though the natural ability of the soul cannot by itself reach the illumination received. Formal locutions have no such basis, but come purely from outside, whether the spirit is recollected or not. An example is the angel speaking to Daniel. Substantial locutions are like formal ones, except that a substantial word is a powerful impression upon the soul from God of a simple form such as 'Love me' or 'Seek goodness'. This is the word of God that said to Abraham, 'Walk in my presence and be perfect'; it is the word of Christ in the Gospel performing miracles. Such words are life and strength and blessing to the soul.

Spiritual feelings are of two kinds. One concerns the affections of the will and relates not directly to the understanding but to the will. This needs to be considered when tackling the purgation of the will. (St John does not in fact return to this issue.) Some sublime touches of this kind are distinct and quickly gone; others less distinct and last longer. Both can cause knowledge to overflow into the understanding as a sublime perception of God, beyond description. The other spiritual feeling is in the substance of the soul. Like that in the affection of the will, it is received passively, neither desired nor planned, as a touch of union, given by God to a soul which is humble, resigned and detached.

Revelations are associated with the spirit of prophecy, and show themselves in two ways. One is intellectual knowledge, comprehending with understanding the truths of God, both with regard to God himself and his creation. Thus illumination may occur concerning the attributes of God — his goodness, his omnipotence, his graciousness, and so on — or of his action in the world — prophecy and discernment, e.g. the judgement of Elisha upon Gehazi. The other is the disclosure of hidden secrets, both with regard to the mystery of God himself and to his works — prophecies concerning the future and the interpretation of past events.

The general rule about the dangers of demonic influence and the difficulty in interpreting the knowledge given whether it be from God or Satan or misunderstood through our own weakness, applies to most of these, namely, all forms of visions, successive and formal locutions and all forms of revelation. Therefore all these must be rejected as unreliable, and even more important, unable to bring us to union with God. Only the substantial words, which are positive divine affirmations impressed upon the soul for its good, and spiritual feelings in the substance of the soul, are both beneficial and appropriate in the path to union with God. This is not to say that there is nothing necessarily of value in those we must reject — the examples given prove this is not so. Rather, the overriding point is that such supernatural knowledge, even when from God, does not provide the means to union, and if accepted and allowed to fill the understanding with clear forms of knowledge, actually hinders spiritual progress. Therefore the understanding must detach itself from these and rest in the obscurity and darkness of faith, that true and appropriate means to union with God in the understanding. The only possible additions to this contemplation which can be safely accepted by the spirit are the substantial words and substantial touches of union from spiritual feelings, received passively, humbly, with resignation to the grace of God. All else is at best a hindrance, at worst a demonic stumbling block, causing souls to fall into error and destruction.

However, there is one more point. Some supernatural knowledge, be it sensual or intellectual, be it in corporeal or noncorporeal form, has proved a blessing to the work of the Church and revealed the nature and ways of God to mankind. How are these to continue to benefit the work of redemption without causing shipwreck to the soul which receives them?

What is needed here is the practice of obedience. First, this means submission to the 'sound sense and doctrine' of the Church. There is no place for individual speculations about God and his ways and once we entertain the notion that we are superior to the faith of the Church, then Satan has us in his grip. A typical and common example of deception deriving from this kind of pride is speculation about the date of the second coming. Secondly, obedience requires us to reveal to our director all forms of supernatural knowledge, and to hold nothing back from him, no matter how sublime or demonic or confusing. This is not in order to assess this knowledge with a view to accepting within the soul what is from God — we have already rejected all clear knowledge, detaching the understanding from it so that we rest in the darkness of faith — but in order for the director to gain a true picture of the state of the soul — whether under demonic attack or receiving the blessings of grace — and to see whether what has been revealed, if of God, should be communicated to higher authority as of possible benefit to the faithful at large. Many centres of pilgrimage are founded upon supernatural visions of Our Lady or one of the saints, and while this is not in itself a sign of the holiness or otherwise of the soul who receives it, God is using that person to promote the work of redemption. Thirdly, obedience leads to accepting the director's analysis and following his instructions in all things, so that the soul may move forward with confidence in the darkness of faith, being voided from those forms of knowledge which do not prepare it for union, and being humble and resigned under the influence of substantial words and spiritual feelings in the substance of the soul if they are given to it. The place of wise and discerning directors of souls in the life of the Church and in the spiritual development of souls is crucial. Lack of such skills both weakens the faith of the Church and causes the loss of many souls.

We now move on to consider the active night of the spirit as it pertains to the memory. Because of the close working of the memory with the understanding, the categories of knowledge affecting the latter, already examined, also apply to the former. The first point, by way of reminder, is that the theological virtue of hope grows in the memory as it is voided increasingly during the passive night of the senses of dependence upon the exterior and interior corporeal senses, producing a developing detachment from all forms of knowledge stored in the memory. This is necessary because God has no form or image that can be comprehended by the memory and therefore if the memory is to be united with God it must become more and more detached from all particular knowledge. Such a voiding of the memory can cause oblivion and loss of the ability to remember, causing the soul to be upset and without judgement or sense. We have already referred to this earlier. Such oblivion passes when the memory becomes used to the state of detachment and its powers revive, but in such a way that it is God who is master of them and not our own will. Such souls increasingly remember only what is in accordance with the will of God and find themselves less and less able to force the memory to operate outside his will. For example, remembering requests for prayer will depend progressively upon whether God requires us to pray for such and such a person or not. We shall be moved to do so or not to do so increasingly by the grace of God in the voided memory.

Not to void the memory of all forms of natural knowledge and reflection, derived from the exterior and interior corporeal senses, leads to three evils. Firstly, the mingling of falsehood and imperfection with truth produces temptation to venial sin, since no knowledge is ever complete and perfect. Secondly, demonic influence upon the memory through the senses leads to more serious false knowledge and mortal sin. Thirdly, reliance upon clear knowledge may deprive us of that moral good which restrains the passions and desires, promoting tranquillity, peace and virtue, and that spiritual good, which advances the development of hope through the exchange of what is unstable and comprehensible for what is immutable and incomprehensible. Therefore all forms of clear knowledge and reflection are to be purged from the memory.

What is true of corporeal natural knowledge is also true of corporeal supernatural knowledge in the memory. 'No supernatural forms or knowledge which can be apprehended by the memory are God, and, in order to reach God, the soul must void itself of all that is not God' (*As.* III, 7, 2). Not to do so produces five evils in the spirit.

First, the soul is frequently deceived, both as to the origin of such knowledge, whether from God or Satan, and of its importance or otherwise.

Secondly, the soul is in peril of presumption and pride, exchanging the virtue of hope for the experience of feelings and insights. 'All visions, revelations and feelings coming from

Heaven, and any thoughts that may proceed from these, are of less worth than the least act of humility' (*As.* III, 9, 4).

Thirdly, Satan can tempt the soul supernaturally with false knowledge, raising unruly desires and pleasures and producing spiritual gluttony through sweetness and delights in the senses imitating the things of God.

Fourthly, the soul is hindered from progress towards union with God because supernatural apprehension in the memory, if entertained, weakens the growth of the virtue of hope. We come to expect them to recur and this expectation undermines hope of union with God as our goal.

Fifthly, supernatural knowledge causes the soul to hold a low and unfitting view of God, by accepting what is given as the nature of God himself. What is incomparable and incomprehensible, beyond being described in terms of type or species, that is, the ineffable being of God, is lost to the memory as it attempts to describe God in terms which come from knowledge, which is a purely creaturely assessment through imagery.

Because of all these evils corporeal supernatural knowledge, even when from God, becomes a snare, even a delusion and cause of sin, if accepted by the memory, and therefore all must be rejected, causing the memory to be darkness in the night which encourages the practice of hope.

So far as intellectual natural knowledge in the memory is concerned, we have already dealt with this, pointing out that it must not be sought or retained in contemplation but surrendered in favour of hope in the memory. With regard to intellectual supernatural knowledge in the memory, clear apprehensions may only be recalled if they produce good effects in the spirit. But they are not recalled in order to be savoured and dwelt upon, only to stir up in the spirit its love and knowledge of God. The point here is renewal in the grace received, not desire to cling to the knowledge communicated to the soul. But if the effects are not good, then such knowledge should never be recalled. However, such a distinction does not apply to obscure knowledge — substantial words and spiritual feelings in the substance of the soul — which the spirit should try to recall as often as possible because its effects are greatly beneficial. What is being produced in this case are touches and impressions of union with God, the very goal we are seeking in hope. Such touches of union do not come through any form, image or figure making its impression on the soul, but they come without form, obscure and indistinct, bringing only graces from God such as light, love, joy and renewal of spirit, to be brought about again in the soul whenever remembered by the memory. St John summarizes thus: 'What must be done, then, that the soul may live in the perfect and pure hope of God is that, whensoever these distinct images, forms and notions come to it, it must not rest in them, but must turn immediately to God, voiding the memory of them entirely, with loving affection. It must neither think of these things nor consider them beyond the degree which is necessary for the understanding and performing of its obligations, if they have any concern with these. And this it must do without setting any affections or inclination upon them, so that they produce no effects in the soul. And thus a man must not fail to think and recall that which he ought to know and do, for, provided he preserves no affection or attachments, this will do him no harm' (*As.* III, 15, 2).

With the understanding and the memory voided and detached from spiritual knowledge, we move on to consider the application of the active night of the spirit to the will. This is the test which consolidates all other efforts at detachment, for unless the will is progressively detached from its affections, advances made in the purging of the other two faculties will prove illusory. The purpose of attempting this detachment from the four affections of joy, hope, grief and fear is to conform the will to the will of God in love, so that 'it may no longer be a base, human will but may become a divine will, being made one with the will of God' (*As.* III, 16, 3).

Because St John did not complete his treatise *The Ascent of Mount Carmel*, only one of the four affections, that of joy, is examined in detail in that book, and he does not give any further analysis of the other three affections in any extant manuscripts. However, where one affection resides in the will, the others are there also, and what applies to one applies to all four. This will enable us to consider the affection of joy, and apply what we learn from that to the other three.

Active joy occurs in the will whenever an object gives it satisfaction. As such it is a chosen activity, arising when the soul clearly and distinctly understands why there is a cause for rejoicing, and is free to express itself thus. There is also a passive joy, not within the power of the soul to choose or not, arising in the soul without it clearly and distinctly understanding the reason why it is rejoicing.

Joy, when entirely chosen, may arise from six kinds of good things or blessings, categorized as temporal, natural, sensual, moral, supernatural and spiritual. By assessing their value or otherwise in aiding our journey to union with God, St John gives us a general principle to be applied to them: 'The will must never rejoice save only in that which is to the honour and glory of God; and that the greatest honour we can show him is that of serving him according to evangelical perfection; and any thing that has naught to do with this is of no value and profit to man' (*As.* III, 17, 2).

Temporal joys are of two kinds — wealth, social status, success at work etc., on the one hand, and children, family, marriage, friendship, etc. on the other. Neither of necessity brings a person to sin, but our weakness can cause us to cling to these and to fail God in the process. Both kinds of temporal blessing can be the source of alienating our love from God; therefore we must not rejoice in either, unless it helps us to serve God. Riches and marriage, for example, can be means of serving God, but both can equally lead to joy which brings evil to the soul, through a series of increasingly severe privations, leading to total withdrawal from God.

First, absorption in this joy of temporal blessings leads to a backward movement of the soul on the road to union, producing a certain blunting of the mind with regard to God and a clouding of our judgement.

Secondly, it leads the will to wander off, out of control, accepting greater liberty with regard to temporal things than is desirable, ceasing to concern itself about them, and becoming attached to temporal pleasures so that the soul withdraws from the things of God and the practice of religion. This is the cause of many imperfections, follies and vanity.

Thirdly, this absorption — often called concupiscence — once the second evil is achieved, turns the whole will covetous

97

for worldly things, so that truth and justice are undermined and the will becomes weak, careless and lukewarm for them. The practice of religion becomes a formality or a compulsion or continues out of habit, but there is no love in it. The soul has quite fallen away from God.

Fourthly, evil completes its work by obliterating all attachment to God in the intellectual faculties. Faith, hope and love leave the understanding, the memory and the will, and the soul surrenders itself into the hands of covetousness, forgetting all that God has ever meant to it. Temporal blessings become the idol such a person worships, and if they are lost at this stage can result in serious agitation, despair, emotional disturbance, even suicide.

In contrast, the benefits which we derive by detaching our joy from temporal things include the development of the virtue of generosity, eliminating covetousness, plus freedom of action in the soul, clarity of reason, rest and tranquillity, and a peaceful confidence in God growing out of a will committed in love to the reverence and worship of God. Also, detachment from these temporal blessings means a greater ability to enjoy them because we can now do so without the anxieties caused by attachment to them. We rejoice in such good things with a clear sense of their true worth, because we neither possess them nor are possessed by them. Finally, detachment leaves the will free for God. Such openness of heart enables God to grant the soul favours which more than compensate for the withdrawal of joy from temporal blessings.

Natural blessings are beauty, gracefulness, being attractive, having a good physical constitution and endowment. To rejoice in these for their own sake is vanity. The will must detach itself from the pleasures of natural blessings, paying them no heed, neither hoping for their increase nor grieving their loss. Not to do so produces many evils, derived from pride. We sink into the coarse and sensual by indulging the enjoyment of natural blessings to our serious hurt. In contrast, detachment from them brings the benefits of increasing humility, from which flow many virtues and great freedom from distractions to our love for God.

Sensual blessings are the pleasures of the exterior and interior corporeal senses. To rejoice in these for their own sake is another form of vanity, this time presuming that our senses can bring us to God, who is beyond sense. However, if we void the will of such pleasure, then joy in sensual blessings can be good if it immediately leads the will to rise up to rejoice in God, leaving the senses behind. But we must be cautious not to use prayer and devotion in which we claim to be doing this as in fact a pretext for indulging our joy in sensual things. The spirit must be nourished and satisfied by the Spirit of God; only then will it lack nothing and desire nothing else. The evils already described under temporal and natural blessings apply equally here. Pride, envy and anger, in particular weaken the will in its love for God, and these sins in their myriad forms undermine our detachment, producing in the end the darkening and failure of conscience and spirit. All this results finally in the reduction of spiritual exercises and withdrawal from the sacraments, especially penance and the Eucharist. On the other hand, the blessings of detachment from sensual blessings include the preservation of virtue and the strength of the spirit, the conversion of the sensual into the spiritual and the bestial into the rational; improved judgement, even of the deep things of God; increased benefit from temporal things because they are no longer a threat to the detached will. But, as always, care must be exercised not to presume too much lest the fall be headlong into disaster.

Moral blessings are the virtues, good habits, the doing of works of mercy, keeping the law of God, being a good citizen, actually putting into practice all our good intentions and inclinations. Unlike the preceding three, these blessings contain some merit in themselves, because of their intrinsic worth, bringing peace, tranquillity, the right and orderly exercise of reason through actions consistent with it, so that, humanly speaking, we cannot have better in this life. Therefore we can rejoice in them for their own sake and take pleasure in them directly. But we have a higher purpose than the good life now — we desire to gain eternal life. This being so, our intention of rejoicing in moral blessings must always be for the sake of honouring and serving God through them. Without this all virtues are worthless in the sight of God — good works profit us nothing unless done in faith. We must realize that the value of our good works is not based upon their number or quality, but upon the love for God which inspires them. Thus, with respect to this moral good, we must concentrate all the strength of our will upon God, purging ourselves of all pleasures, consolations and other benefits which good works bring with them. The will should desire that God alone has joy in its good works, and should be content to do them without becoming attached to them. For the evils which come from such attachment are increasing vanity and self-love, resulting in both a halt on the road to perfection and the loss of God's favour. In contrast, the benefits of detachment include freedom from demonic deception, the better performance of good works because we judge the matter in hand more clearly, poverty of spirit, meekness, humility, freedom from spiritual envy, avarice, sloth and gluttony. Detachment from joy in moral blessings gives us the security from which to do good works with confidence to the glory of God alone.

Supernatural blessings are a division of the spiritual blessings to be considered next, but worth a category of their own — these are those gifts from God which by grace transcend natural virtue and capacity, e.g. the gift of wisdom to Solomon, the graces referred to by St Paul, including faith, healing powers, the working of miracles, prophecy, knowledge, discernment of spirits, tongues, etc. These are gifts from God for use in the life of the Church and the world at large. They may produce temporal benefits, e.g. through miraculous healing, plus spiritual and eternal benefits insofar as they make God known to those who receive them or see them. The temporal benefit merits little or no rejoicing on our part — it is a gift from God not our own merit at work — and indeed such supernatural gifts may be exercised by people not in a state of grace or charity, e.g. Balaam, Solomon, Simon Magus. Therefore, we should not rejoice in them because of any temporal benefit, but only if we reap the spiritual benefit, which is serving and loving God through supernatural blessings, by using them for his glory. Desire to do the will of God alone is the required condition in which the will is called to exercise these gifts with safety. Detachment from them is essential lest the following evils ensue: self-deception, loss of faith and boasting. The benefits of detachment, in contrast, are deliverance from these three evils, the development of the desire to praise and rejoice in God, and the lifting up of the soul itself from all desire for signs and wonders, so that God may increase its faith, hope and love by infusing the soul with these virtues supernaturally. This benefit leads directly towards the perfect union of the soul with God.

Spiritual blessings proper are those gifts from God which are not for general use but are to do with God and the soul alone. These are two kinds of communication from God — one is delectable, the other painful; each can be received in two ways — clearly and distinctly understood and in a dark, confused form. The painful ones apply to the passive night of the spirit, and will be dealt with later. Also, we must distinguish between the faculties of the spirit by saying that spiritual blessings are enjoyed in the area of knowledge with regard to the understanding, imagination with regard to the memory and the affections with regard to the will.

The same principle applies to the attitude of the will towards clear and distinct spiritual blessings of a delectable kind in the understanding and memory as the latter practice on the clear supernatural knowledge they receive. The will should not joy in these, but detach itself, taking care to maintain itself free from the pleasures that these spiritual blessings bring. This applies to all supernatural knowledge that is clear and distinct — it should never be entertained and enjoyed in the will lest it fall into the errors already set out at length that befall a will which falls short of love for God.

With regard to these delectable spiritual blessings in a clear, distinct form which are apprehended by the will through the affections, they fall into four kinds, the motive, provocative, both of which St John describes, and two others not described in the unfinished *The Ascent of Mount Carmel*. The two described refer to statues, churches, oratories etc., and to preachers, both in respect of the hearers and the preacher himself. In both cases, we are to avoid any clinging to them, setting the affections on them. Any grace received through them comes through the spirit receiving what it sees or hears with faith and penitence, exciting the will to deepen its love for God. But we are not to go around making special attachments to particular places, things or preachers, lest we detach our love from God and attach it to them because of the benefit we have received through them. Reliance upon these can only lead to partiality, inconstancy, dependence on place and person, indulging of the will upon sensible devotion and failure to renounce our own will for that of the will of God. Special places of grace no doubt exist and we should go to them, but inwardly we must be detached from them and seek only to be there in the darkness of faith, voided in hope and dedicated in love to God. Anything less than this and we are in danger of falling away from that desire to conform our will to God's will, in the detachment of spirit which he requires.

St John does not expound the other two delectable spiritual blessings apprehended by the will. No doubt they are analogous to locutions and spiritual feelings in the understanding, and when clear and distinct should be treated in the same way as the motive and provocative, that is, in a totally detached manner.

Neither does he expound in *The Ascent of Mount Carmel* the attitude we need to take to active joy in the dark, confused form of delectable spiritual blessings, though, by analogy with the dark knowledge of faith which we call contemplation with regard to the understanding, we may surmise that such dark, confused forms, can be admitted as aids to the will to persist in the practice of contemplation. It is joy in God as the ineffable goal of the soul's efforts as it reorientates the intellectual faculties on the theological virtues. Because this joy does not convey distinct knowledge which would undermine faith and hope, but only increases the strength of the will to love God by directing this affection to that end, it can be recalled and revived whenever required to maintain the practice of contemplation in the detachment of this dark night of the spirit.

Neither does St John refer again in *The Ascent of Mount Carmel* to passive joy, though the terminology would imply that it is a joy which is of God, not the soul, entering the will without preparation, an involuntary joy, analogous to intellectual supernatural knowledge in the understanding. Providing such joy is related to knowledge without clear form, like spiritual feelings

102

in the substance of the soul, it can be accepted and becomes a source of strength in the will as it rejoices to love God alone. If, however, it is accompanied by clear knowledge of any kind, such joy may be entertained only if we do not cling to the clear knowledge recalled, lest it hinder our progress towards union of the will with God in love. If we are tempted to cling to such knowledge, then it is better not to recall it and seek to renew any joy there might be in it.

St John does not analyse the attitude of the will to the affection of hope, but because the affections tend to work together and be present together, we may assume that his analysis would be the same as that towards joy. Active hope for temporal, natural, sensual blessings should always be voided in the will as damaging to spiritual progress; hope for moral and supernatural blessings is only permissible if it is solely for the glory of God, but detachment is necessary from them lest they become obstacles also; hope for delectable spiritual blessings of a clear and distinct kind, applied to all three intellectual faculties, remains a danger to the soul and must be voided; only hope for the dark confused form of delectable spiritual blessings can be encouraged in the will as a further support in maintaining the will in its task of loving God alone within the darkness of contemplation. Passive hope, similarly can be accepted if it is without clear form, but is to be rejected if accompanied by clear knowledge of any kind, to which we are tempted to cling.

Because the affections of grief and fear as the negative consequence of joy and hope tend to operate only when the soul is attached to joy and hope, detachment from these latter, except when permitted in the limited cases set out above, should remove any tendency for grief and fear, operating naturally, to affect the will adversely in its love for God. If however this is not so then these painful affections will make havoc in the will. The way to tackle these is the positive rejection of joy and hope, with penitence as necessary, rather than seeking to contain grief and fear without first rejecting the other two. However grief and fear can produce painful communications in their own right and these will be tackled during the passive night of the spirit, which we now consider.

8. The Path to Union: Journey's End

The passive night of the spirit is the third and last 'ligature' or gateway to be gone through by the soul on the way to union with God. It is the most terrible and painful of all three and most souls do not reach this point during their earthly life — it is a kind of purgatory, beyond which is spiritual betrothal and spiritual marriage. Most of us spend the mature years of Christian obedience within the active night of the spirit developing the virtues of faith, hope and love in the intellectual faculties by contemplation; detaching ourselves from those clear and distinct forms of knowledge and active affections of joy and hope which distract and undermine this process; and stabilizing the practice of contemplation with the aid of active joy and hope towards the obscure spiritual blessings which come from God and increase our love for him. Some of us, but not all, may experience touches of union in the soul by means of substantial words or spiritual feelings in the substance of the soul in the understanding, and by recalling them in the memory, and by receiving passive joys and hopes of an obscure form in the will. Only very few are asked by God to go further into the third 'ligature' which intensifies the darkness, seems to undermine all progress made so far, and causes severe pain to body and soul.

The reason for this third 'night' lies in the fact that the soul in the active night of the spirit is using its intellectual faculties in an active manner to turn the spirit away from paths which distract into the path of dark, loving knowledge found in contemplation. As such, the resolve of the will to hold fast to this course is necessary and that resolve is buttressed by active joy and hope towards dark, obscure spiritual blessings. There is still such activity within the spirit that the soul only experiences, at most, touches of union of an unstable kind. To experience permanent union with God requires the further quietening of the soul by detaching it from the activity of the understanding, memory and will in the practice of faith, hope and love — God's grace is pulling down old props for the third time — and causing it to rest entirely in God. The means by which God does this is by sending painful communications to us through the affections of grief and fear which now assault the soul. The intellectual faculties cease to operate. The soul is plunged into severe pain and deepest darkness. All appears lost with no hope of recovering what was before. The only way ahead is forward into the pain and the darkness, with all the fear that entails.

The justification for this step of bringing the intellectual faculties into passivity is as follows: although the senses have been purified, the pleasures of the spirit deriving from the senses in a spiritual manner cause fatigue. The sensitive part of the soul remains weak and cannot experience the strong things of the spirit required for union. This is the root cause of all raptures, trances, dislocations, and such things have to be left behind before progress to union can be made. Further, the soul still retains imperfections — imperfect habits and affections rooted in the spirit, and therefore unable to be purged completely during the passive night of the senses, plus actual sins, weaknesses and follies varying from the slight to the highly deceptive from Satan — which cause the spirit to fail to protect itself adequately from the influence of visions, revelations, locutions and feelings. These the soul is often tempted to accept and retain. Further, since all habits, good and bad, find their strength in the spirit, the passive night of the senses can only correct and restrain sensual desire rather than completely purge it, and it is not until all habits are purged in the spirit that the disturbances of sense can be thoroughly eliminated. God is finally doing to death the old Adam in us so that we can be clothed with the life of the new man, Jesus Christ. God 'strips the faculties, affections and feelings, both spiritual and sensual, both outward and inward, leaving the understanding dark, the will dry, the memory empty and the affections in the deepest affliction, bitterness and straitness, taking from the soul the pleasure and experience of spiritual blessings which it had aforetime, so that this privation may be one of the principles which are required in the spirit that the spiritual form of the spirit may be introduced into it and united with it, which is the union of love' (*Dk.Nt.* II, 3, 3).

We are now in God's hand. We can do nothing but receive passively what he sends, accepting the pain as readily as the former pleasures now done away. The pain comes because, as the darkness of contemplation deepens without the support of the active affections of the will, the grace of God begins to purge us of our imperfections, which cannot coexist in our spirit along with perfect love given to the soul by God. Also, the infusion of divine love causes pain at first because it is in itself an attack on those imperfect habits and actions — they are being driven out of the soul. Thirdly, the soul is still naturally, morally and spiritually weak and suffers violence at the hands of divine love as a great burden crushing it. This leads the soul to think that it has fallen out of favour with God, causing it to experience grief and fear. Such chastising is not immediately recognized as a sign of God's mercy and favour towards it, but only sore affliction and punishment. In addition, since this is a passive state, it is God who acts and the soul who receives, and although God's purpose is to transfigure the soul by grace into becoming divine also, the actual experience of the soul itself is of being destroyed spiritually. Lastly, consciousness within the soul of the majesty and power of God, and by implication, the greatness of the demand God is making of it, contrasts painfully with awareness of its own poverty of spirit and wretchedness. Temporal, natural and spiritual blessings all vanish and the soul is left in the midst of the privation their absence brings. God is purging the sensual part in aridity, the faculties through emptiness and the spirit by deepest thick darkness. Sometimes, in addition, external evils attack the body through persecution, misunderstanding, rejection, calumny, etc., which we must bear with resigned indifference and love.

The will in particular suffers terribly, recalling past evils and fearing they have no remedy, remembering former consolations and grieving that happiness has been lost for ever. At this stage, the director must not produce facile explanations or suggest routes of escape from the pain — the soul will not believe him and he will cause it only further sorrow and confusion. The truth is that until God has completed the purging of the soul there is no means of relieving this affliction; the length of time and the severity of the purging depends upon the strength of the imperfections present and the weakness of the soul faced with receiving infused love. Usually, to be effective, it lasts for some years, although there may be times of relief when the assault on the soul ceases to cause pain and becomes a loving assault, full of sweetness and peace. But such interludes are not to be taken as the end of the period of trial — suffering returns and plunges the soul deeper than ever before. Most who go through this period — which is analogous to the period of the passive night of the senses when snatches of contemplation give easement to the sufferings of the soul at that level — have severe misgivings whether it will ever end. Even realizing that they now have great love for God is no consolation. This is what St John calls spiritual betrothal and it is a period of instability and danger for the unwary soul. During this time it is vital that the soul realizes and holds fast to the truth that its suffering is not the fault of God. 'In contemplation and the divine inflowing, there is naught that of itself can cause affliction, but that they rather cause great sweetness and delight.... The cause is rather the weakness and imperfection from which the soul then suffers, and the dispositions which it has in itself and which make it unfit for the reception of them' (Dk.Nt. II, 9, 11). God will not give us evil things, because he is all goodness — rather the suffering comes from our inability at this stage to receive the fullness of love he is bestowing upon us.

With this acceptance in the soul, it is fired increasingly deeply with love for God. Insofar as this love is infused, it is passive rather than active, and so has touches of union in it because the action is God's, not the soul's, which rests passively, subdued to God's grace. As we get used to these touches so the love which God infuses in the soul finds us more able and ready to receive it, more prepared to unite our will to it, more recollected to benefit from it, and more withdrawn from and less able to enjoy anything else in heaven or earth. What begins without the soul's awareness becomes increasingly perceived by the soul and a great longing is set up for the love of God. We grow in capacity to receive the love given to us.

Through the image of fire, producing light and heat, St John describes the fire of love as sometimes illuminating the understanding and sometimes enkindling the will, sometimes both together. Thus there are times when the spirit understands what God is doing to it but the will is arid; on other occasions the will burns with a passion of love but the understanding is empty; yet again, both may benefit and all suffering is done away.

The movement of divine grace in the soul gradually leads it by love through the purging away of all imperfections and weaknesses, and the last vestiges of demonic interference, from spiritual betrothal into a stable union in which the soul is perfected passively by infused love and is satisfied in the sublime favours of God in spiritual marriage.

However, even at this late stage, Satan is able to make limited forays against the soul. He cannot use his influence over the animal soul, which is his usual means of entry, to create havoc in the spirit, because the contemplative state of spiritual betrothal is infused into the soul passively and without the knowledge or operation of the exterior and interior corporeal sense. But Satan, although deprived of entry at this level, now attacks the will through supernatural actions upon the affections of grief and fear, stirring up in the soul passively and without its consent all sorts of afflictions, causing terror and horror. Here we have a demonic assault, designed to put within the soul, passively received, the ultimate deception, namely, that God brings evil upon those who love him. This is not so. It is Satan who seeks to cast us down into unbelief through the deepening of our grief and fear into despair and rejection of God. But, as always, the difference between the grace of God and the influence of Satan is that, although both are supernatural, the former brings only goodness to us, which we receive passively, and its benefit persists without any effort on our part, whereas the latter brings distress and anxiety which only persists if we actively receive and entertain it. Satan cannot penetrate to the fullest recesses of the soul without our acquiescence, and therefore when the soul is assaulted with passive griefs and fears from Satan, it must stand fast, resisting his onslaught, denying the deception he is planting in the soul. This is enough to blunt the attack, and without knowing how it happens, we discover that the soul becomes detached and is drawn into a deeper peace and joy, leaving the temptations outside, unable to do damage to the love that is between us and God.

However, there is one further level of demonic attack on the soul which St John calls 'a greater affliction to it than any torment in this life could be' (*Dk.Nt.* II, 23, 9). He finds it difficult to describe except as 'this horrible communication (passing) direct from spirit to spirit, in something like nakedness and clearly distinguished from all that is corporeal...grievous beyond what every sense can feel' (*Dk.Nt.* II, 23, 9). Although this may last some time, it is never for a long time, because it would cause the dissolution of the person. But when it has gone, the memory of it remains, causing terrible affliction. God permits this last terror in order finally 'to purify the soul and to prepare it by means of this spiritual vigil for some great spiritual favour and festival which he desires to grant it, for he never mortifies save to give life, neither humbles save to exalt, which comes to pass shortly afterwards' (*Dk.Nt.* II, 23, 10). The blessing now granted to the soul is 'a wondrous and delectable spiritual contemplation, sometimes so lofty that there is no language to describe it...for these spiritual visions belong to the next life rather than to this, and when one is seen this is a preparation for the next' (*Dk.Nt.* II, 23, 10).

This exalted state is the final transfiguration of the soul with divine love, causing it to become divine itself in all its powers and faculties, totally conformed in peace and tranquillity to the loving will of God. 'That which God communicates to the soul in this most intimate union is completely ineffable, so that naught can be said thereof, even as naught can be said concerning God himself which may describe him; for it is God himself who communicates this to the soul, and transforms her into himself with marvellous glory, so that they are both in one...this communication from God (is) diffused substantially in the entire soul, or, to express it better, the soul is more nearly transformed into God according to its substance and its spiritual faculties. According to the understanding it drinks wisdom and knowledge; according to the will, it drinks sweetest love; and, according to the memory, it drinks recreation and delight in the remembrance and sense of glory' (*Sp.Cant.* XVII, 3-4).

St Augustine describes the human race without faith in these terms: 'O God, you have made us for yourself and our hearts are restless till they rest in you.' He also describes our transfigured state when we attain to union with God in heaven thus: 'There we shall rest, and we shall see; we shall see and we shall love; we shall love and we shall praise. Behold what shall be in the end, and shall not end.' St John of the Cross leads us from that restlessness of heart with which we all start to that perfect rest for which we are all created. In so doing, he opens up for all who follow his teaching a sure and certain way to union with God, to the transfiguration of ourselves by God, and to the promise of eternal life, now and hereafter, in God.

Let the last word be with St John of the Cross himself. Describing our recreation through union with God in terms which recall the language of the Genesis story of creation, he writes thus: 'It is as if a man awakened and breathed; the soul is conscious of a rare delight in the breathing of the Holy Spirit in God, in whom it is glorified and enkindled in love.... Of that breathing of God, which is full of blessing and glory and of the delicate love of God for the soul, I should not wish to speak, neither do I desire now to speak; for I see clearly that I cannot say aught concerning it, and that, were I to speak of it, it would not appear as great as it is. For it is a breathing of God himself into the soul, wherein, through that awakening of lofty knowledge of Deity, the Holy Spirit breathes into the soul according to the understanding and knowledge which it has had of God, who inspires it with divine delicacy and glory, according to that which it has seen in God; for, his breathing being full of blessing and glory, the Holy Spirit has filled the soul with blessing and glory, wherein he has inspired it with love for himself, which transcends all description and all sense, in the deep things of God, to whom be honour and glory. Amen' (*Lvg.Fl.* 16-17).

LAUS DEO

Bibliography

The Spirituality of the New Testament and the Fathers, Louis Bouyer (Burns & Oates Ltd, 1960)

Introduction to Spirituality, Louis Bouyer (Darton, Longman & Todd Ltd, 1961)

Western Mysticism: Neglected Chapters in the History of Religion, Dom Cuthbert Butler OSB (Constable & Company Ltd, 1922)

The Spiritual Letters of Dom John Chapman OSB (Sheed & Ward, 1959)

The Cloud of Unknowing, Anon, trans. Clifton Wolters (Penguin, 1961)

The Life of St John of the Cross, Crisógno de Jesús OCD (Longmans, 1958)

The Crucible of Love. A Study of the Mysticism of St Teresa of Jesus and St John of the Cross, E.W. Trueman Dicken (Darton, Longman & Todd Ltd, 1963)

Dionysius the Areopagite on the Divine Names and the Mystical Theology, trans. C.E. Rolt (SPCK, 1920)

The Rule of Saint Albert, Bede Edwards ODC (Aylesford & Kensington Carmels, 1973)

Sinai and Carmel: The Biblical Roots of the Spiritual Doctrine of St John of the Cross, Fr Fabrizio Foresti ODC (Darlington Carmel, 1981)

Spirit of Flame. A Study of St John of the Cross, E. Allison Peers (SCM Press Ltd, 1943)

The Complete Works of St John of the Cross, trans. and ed. E. Allison Peers (Burns, Oates & Washbourne Ltd, 1947)